SKYSCRAPER

First published in the United Kingdom in 2003 by
Thames & Hudson Ltd, 181A High Holborn, London WC1V 7QX

www.thameshudson.com

© 2003 Universe Publishing
Text © Eric Höweler

British Library Cataloguing-in-Publication Data
A catalogue record for this book is available from the British Library

ISBN 0-500-28446-6

Printed and bound in Italy

SKYSCRAPER

DESIGNS OF THE RECENT PAST AND FOR THE NEAR FUTURE

ERIC HÖWELER

Thames & Hudson

contents

preface

william pedersen

Mr. Höweler's book documents an important milestone in the development of the tall building. It comes at a time when the tall building is evolving from its almost universal perception as an instrument of financial speculation into the more mature realization that it alone will enable us to achieve the urban densities necessary to live sustainably on this planet.

Ironically, all the architects view themselves as urbanists yet many still show limited interest in the modern city's most dominant component: the tall building. For them it is viewed as a financial instrument for commercial exploitation. Shorn of social and cultural value, the inescapable link between the tall building and commerce dulls the self-proclaimed artist-architect's passion for the building type. Perhaps Cass Gilbert did start the era of the tall building off on the wrong foot by calling it "a machine which makes the land pay." His rhetoric did not impede his artistic impulse, however, as the magnificent Woolworth Building attests.

As we enter the twenty-first century, each passing year brings more evidence in support of the environmental fragility of this planet we live on. World demographics call for the doubling of our population in the next forty years, with the greatest majority of this explosion occurring in Asia. If the human race is to survive, we must live, if for sustainable reasons alone, more densely. Per capita, the world's densest cities like New York, Tokyo, and Hong Kong are also its most energy-efficient. The present density of these models will appear bucolic in comparison to the world's greatest cities at the end of the twenty-first century. Similarly, the present size and scale of tall buildings will look diminutive. Seen through the lens of necessity the tall building will no longer be viewed as an instrument of exploitation and dubious social responsibility. It will be transformed into a vehicle that enables the sustainability of our planet.

Throughout the world all major cities are now dominated by the tall building. However, only a relatively small percentage of these tall buildings can indeed call themselves "skyscrapers." Absolute height is not in itself a determinant or a qualification for the term. A proportional relationship of height to width, pointing to the very slender, is a more useful indicator. Even this is not a guarantee. Rather, for me, a skyscraper is defined by an aspiration, one that intends to link earth and sky. Therefore, by this definition, a relatively short building, such as the Woolworth Building, is a skyscraper. To my eyes, Hong Kong has more skyscrapers than New York. I view central Hong Kong almost as a fertile valley surrounded by mountains. The tall buildings appear to be growing like plant material from the forest floor, each striving like mad for the light and the sky. New York, it has been said, is more of a "deep" city, a city where the street grid appears to be excavated into solid material. The buildings emerge from this act of excavation.

Among tall buildings, only skyscrapers have the potential to create an iconic presence which can symbolize, or come to symbolize, a city. During the early part of the twentieth century it was predicted that an "international style" of architecture would emerge bringing the world's cities towards greater homogeneity. It is hard to deny that the tall building has been instrumental in accomplishing this to a substantial degree. Yet, as global competition among cities increases, there has come about an increasing desire to differentiate cities one from another. It is a trend, as Mr. Höweler identifies, towards "glocaliza-tion," "towards the specific, the local, and authentic." If skyscrapers can play a meaningful role in this phenomenon, their designers face the complex challenge of drawing the meaning, or the overlay of meaning, they wish to impart directly from the place the building is to inhabit. Given all of the universal elements contained within the building type, this quest for local meaning is a substantial challenge. Ideally, architecture has the capacity to link the past, the present, and the future. Multidirectional temporal linkage requires symbolic representation which is sufficiently "open-ended" to enable multiple readings and to avoid freezing a culture in time. All of these issues are identified by Mr. Höweler in this book. The clarity of his classifications within the building type achieves a useful perspective for delineating its evolution. He has crafted a benchmark for those of us who are struggling to bring about the formal and urbanistic potential of tall buildings. Assuming its new mantle of social responsibility the tall building will acquire a higher status as a subject for theoretical and artistic debate. It is destined to be the most highly discussed building type of its era. This book is an extraordinary beginning to this conversation.

vertical now:
the skyscraper at the beginning of the 21st century

eric höweler

The skyscraper, more than any other building type, has the capacity to capture the public imagination. Its sheer scale, visual prominence, and symbolic potential have rendered it a speculative enterprise, economically, technologically, and architecturally. The skyscraper and the urban skyline have become iconic representations of cities around the world. From New York to Kuala Lumpur, London to Hong Kong, and Singapore to Sao Paolo, skyscrapers define the image of the metropolis. The skyscraper is representative of urbanity, of density, of modernity—in short, of the driving forces of the twentieth century. It occupies the intersection of real estate, finance, technology, social aspirations, and cultural sensibilities, and, as a cultural artifact, serves as an architecturally condensed index of the present moment—vertical now.

As the preeminent building type of the last century, the skyscraper presents a unique challenge to architects and architecture. Historians and critics look to architecture to "take the temperature of the age," chronicling as it does the evolution of design styles:

modernism, postmodernism, functionalism, minimalism, and supermodernism.[1] The skyscraper's positioning—between form and finance, architectural style and technological necessity, visionary concept and social utility—makes it a powerful indicator of cultural and economic conditions. The skyscraper has been called a "social condenser" and a "vertical machine," and yet it has traditionally been seen as a building type outside the mainstream of architectural culture. Despite its close relationship to development forces, the skyscraper has created a provocative and unique range of architectural approaches to its design. Perhaps because of those very ties, it serves as a barometer of contemporary culture.

ALCHEMY

The skyscraper is an alchemical mix of real estate speculation, technological advancements, and architectural experimentation. At the dawn of the twentieth century, industrialization, urban growth, and speculative development combined with innovations such as steel framing, fireproofing, and the passen-

fig 1 Metropolitan Life Insurance Building, 1909.

ger elevator. Buildings rose to unprecedented heights, and expanded to unprecedented dimensions, creating rentable office space where none had existed previously. The birth of the skyscraper created a new speculative terrain of vertical extension.

Cass Gilbert, the architect of the Woolworth building, declared the skyscraper "a machine that makes the land pay." Market forces, including vacancy rates and economic outlook, determine the space necessary to produce a return on investment. Specifics of typical lease depth, the integration of information technology, as well as zoning laws and land use patterns, further shape the design of the tall office building. These determinants are what Carol Willis has called "vernaculars of capitalism," that have shaped the skylines of cities through their impact on skyscraper design.[2]

New technologies are transforming the skyscraper by pushing the limits of how high and how fast they can be built. Architects and engineers constantly strive to advance the structural limits of what can be erected, while construction costs and market demand accelerate the speed at which skyscrapers are built. Material developments like high-strength concrete allow for taller and lighter structures. New techniques in construction allow for foundations to be built on sites previously considered unbuildable. In Hong Kong, where time and space come at a spectacular cost, "top-down" construction allows a building to be built up from the ground and down into the earth simultaneously, reducing the overall construction time. New requirements for information technologies are determining the floor-to-floor heights in office buildings, and wireless communication is transforming the contemporary workplace.

DESIGN

The skyscraper represents extremely fine-tuned architecture. It is calibrated to market forces and technological efficiencies. The skyscraper is also representative of architectural attitudes and trends. Debates about the appropriate stylistic expression for the tall building date back to its earliest days, when Louis Sullivan declared that the tall office building "must be every inch a proud and soaring thing, rising in sheer exaltation that from top to bottom is a unit without a single dissenting line."[3]

Early skyscraper designs looked to past building styles and materials to guide the design of the new structures. Pierre LeBrun's 1909 design for the Metropolitan Life Insurance building borrows the profile of the campanile of St. Mark's Cathedral in Venice. *[fig 1]* Cass Gilbert's 1913 Woolworth building employs a Gothic language of attenuated vertical lines and an ornamental crown to dress the new steel-framed skeleton. *[fig 2]* Historical eclecticism was the pervasive strategy during the early days of skyscraper design. Architects borrowed the campanile, the cathedral, and the column, stretching, stacking, and scaling them into uncanny compositions. The process of design became a process of translation, from one building type to another.[4]

The 1922 design competition for the *Chicago Herald Tribune* building illustrates a pivotal moment in the evolution of skyscraper design. The competition called for the most "beautiful and distinctive office building in the world." The extreme variety of entries reflects a lack of consensus on the appropriate style for the new typology of the tall office building. The competition recorded a unique moment in architecture, a virtual inventory of the moment, "when the long classical tradition was poised on the edge of the unknown abyss of modernism."[5] The competition entries serve as a measure of the age, recording one of the greatest moments of stylistic diversity and transformation.

The winning entry, a Gothic-inspired tower complete with flying buttresses, was designed by Howells and Hood. *[fig 3]* However, it was the second-place entry by Eliel Saarinen, a vertically articulated setback tower, that was to have a greater impact on the evolution of the skyscraper. *[fig 4]* Within ten years the decorative language of the winning entry had fallen out of favor, and its architect, Raymond Hood, was designing skyscrapers in what became known as the International Style. Hood's streamlined design for the McGraw Hill building in 1932, expressive of the building's non-loadbearing facade, was an early benchmark for modern architecture.

Following World War II, the rise of American business and the influence from European architects found its logical architectural expression in American modernism, which married the requirements for large volumes of office space with notions of mass production and the expression of technology. Skidmore Owings & Merrill's Lever House and Mies van der Rohe's Seagram Building, with their abstract massing, streamlined facades, and urban plazas, had a tremendous impact on skyscraper design, sparking derivative designs in most major American cities. *[fig 6]*

Referential strategies reemerged with postmodern architecture in the 1970s, after several decades of streamlined modernism. Intent on recuperating the humanistic elements of architecture feared lost in modernism, postmodern architects experimented with a parade of historical references and citations.[6] Philip Johnson's provocative design for the AT&T building, a broken-pediment-topped Manhattan skyscraper, ignited a debate about modernism, materials, and meaning that lasted through the mid 1990s. *[fig 7]*

In the last twenty years, architectural design trends have come full circle: architects embraced postmodernism's historical referentiality as a rejection of modernism's stark abstractions, only to then reject postmodernism's whimsical historical appropriations and embrace minimalism's refined lines, and once again to a recuperation of the structural expression of the building technology.

SPECTRUM

This book provides a survey of contemporary skyscraper designs, ranging from the highly decorative, referential designs of C. Y. Lee in Taiwan to the articulated high-tech designs by Norman Foster in Frankfurt to Kohn Pedersen Fox's sculptural and abstract skyscrapers planned for Shanghai to the dynamic forms of Coop Himmelb(l)au's buildings in Vienna to the diverse and ecologically sensitive projects developed by Ken Yeang in Malaysia. Together they represent a spectrum of contemporary skyscraper design.

The designs fall into several distinct but overlapping groupings that are characterized by a common set of issues or concerns. Some of these issues, like expression of structural systems, are part of an ongoing debate among architects. Other concerns address emerging preoccupations with the ecological impact of building. These groupings are not meant as new categories or styles, but rather as convergences of

fig 2 Cass Gilbert's Woolworth Building, 1913.

fig 3 Howells and Hood's gothic-inspired first-place competition entry for the Chicago World Tribune tower.

fig 4 Eliel Saarinen's second-place entry was to have a greater impact on the evolution of the skyscraper.

fig 5 Adolf Loos's proposal, in the shape of a Doric column, makes reference to the skyscraper's classical origins.

design approaches or strategies: Global/Local, High-Tech, Monolithic, Kinetic, Scenographic, Mediatic, and Ecological. I have avoided a purely chronological approach because, as we have seen, design strategies tend to fade and reemerge. Organized in this manner, the uncanny juxtapositions and parallels that emerge across historical styles are brought into focus.

"Global/Local" skyscrapers are an emergent phenomenon in which the forces of globalization and homogenization create a turn towards the specific, the local, and the authentic. The strategy employed by these designs is to overlay elements of traditional or vernacular building traditions on conventional structural frames to relate the building to its context. "High-Tech" skyscrapers express and celebrate the technology that enables them. With strategies such as structural expression and the articulation of component assemblies, systems-driven towers continue to change with advances in technology.

The "Monolithic" skyscraper transforms a powerful and expressive gesture into a highly sculptural and singular form. Often the expression of structure and enclosure are subdued to allow the reading of the overall gesture. "Kinetic" skyscraper designs express a dynamic process of movement and transformation in their static forms, while projects under the heading of "Scenographic" address uses of architecture and imagery, and the increasing tendency of architecture to participate in the spectacle of the contemporary city. The theatrical dimension of the skyscraper is exploited as a singular urban protagonist, or as a scenic backdrop for architectural fantasies. "Mediatic" refers to a new category of buildings that have incorporated new mass-media and display technologies, rendering their facades as surfaces for mass communication. A concern with the impact of human activity on the environment has sponsored a group of "Ecological" skyscrapers that consciously engage issues of sustainability and land use.

Lastly, I have included a number of projects that have emerged as responses to the events of September 11, 2001. The tragic event, and the void that it created, prompted a series of proposals for how to rethink and rebuild that particular site. Many of the designs included skyscrapers, some designed to be taller than the original Twin Towers.

SURVEY

This book presents a panoramic spectrum of skyscraper designs at the beginning of the twenty-first century. This survey of the contemporary vertical landscapes of skyscraper design suggests a diverse and uneven terrain, where there is no single dominant style, ideology, or doctrine. Instead, a multiplicity of attitudes, positions, and architectural styles constitute vertical now. As the skyscraper continues to play an increasingly important role in the evolution of cities, we can begin to trace the contours of a broad spectrum of architectural sensibilities and cultural attitudes. Just as the 1922 *Chicago Herald Tribune* competition served as an architectural measure of the age, the hope is that the following collection will serve as a similar document—recording the dramatic and diverse range of design strategies and cultural attitudes of the present.

1 The architectural historian Charles Jencks, who is credited with popularizing the term *postmodernism*, maps the stylistic evolution of contemporary architecture, as styles and –isms merge and transform, assuming pseudo-scientific nomenclatures: postmodern space, layering and ambiguity, dissonant collage, folding, cybernetic, biomorphic, etc. in Charles Jencks, *The New Paradigm in Architecture*, Yale University Press, New Haven, 2002, p. 50, and Hans Ibelings, *Supermodernism: Architecture in the Age of Globalization*, NAI Publishers, Rotterdam, 1998.

2 Carol Willis, *Form Follows Finance: Skyscrapers and Skylines in New York and Chicago*, Princeton Architectural Press, New York, 1995.

3 Louis H. Sullivan, *Kindergarten Chats and Other Writings*, Dover Publications, New York, 1979, p. 206.

4 For an account of the various strategies of translation, from stacking to stretching, see Robert Twombly's essay, "The Skyscraper as Icon, 1890–1920," in *Power + Style: A Critique of Twentieth-Century Architecture in the United States*, Hill and Wang, New York, 1995.

5 Ada Louise Huxtable, *The Tall Building Artistically Reconsidered: The Search for a Skyscraper Style*, University of California Press, Berkeley, 1982, p. 33.

6 "The examples of history, respectable again after half a century of denial, are being mined for nostalgia, novelty, and innuendo," Ada Louise Huxtable, Ibid., p. 9.

fig 6 Mies van der Rohe's Seagram Building.

fig 7 The AT&T Building, designed by Philip Johnson.

global / local

The impact of globalization on the built environment is manifested in the explosive growth of cities around the world and the proliferation of the skyscraper as a ubiquitous building type. The forces of communication, migration, business, and technology are rapidly erasing borders, eroding former geographic and cultural divides, and creating urban conditions that are common to many cities. It is increasingly difficult to identify the purely local or the purely global. The term "glocal" reflects the condition where the two terms, global and local, operate simultaneously. "Glocal" architecture articulates the complex nature of this contemporary cultural condition.

In his 1983 essay entitled "Critical Regionalism: Six Points for an Architecture of Resistance," Kenneth Frampton identifies regionalism as a viable strategy for addressing the criticisms of the modern movement, while addressing the complexities of a cross-cultural architectural practice. His argument called for architecture to play a mediating role between the homogenizing effects of the universal and the specificities of the local. "The fundamental strategy of Critical Regionalism is to mediate the impact of universal civilization with elements derived indirectly from the

fig 1 The T&C Tower is one of a new breed of self-consciously Chinese skyscrapers emerging as the skyscraper goes global.

fig 2 The Grand 50 Tower seeks to mediate between local culture and a universal building type—the skyscraper.

particularities of a particular place."¹ For many architects, Frampton's regionalism provided the model for a global practice suited to modern building types and sensitive to diverse contexts.

The coexistence and mutual mutability of the global and the local have brought the question of regionalism to the foreground. While geographic borders have remained in place, a "glocal" culture has created a new interconnectedness of place, community, and identity. Singular cartographies of culture have grown faint. Modern technology and mass media have created more fluid communities that coexist within a diverse global, national, civic, and ethnic context.

Contemporary trends in architectural practice register an increase in international commissions, particularly for a building type requiring specialized technical expertise, such as the skyscraper. With the increase in transnational practices and international commissions, design strategies for high-rise buildings need to address issues of symbolism, identity, and site specificity. The glocal skyscraper is one trend that attempts to mediate and articulate the complex negotiations between universal building type and local cultural associations. Given the enormous symbolic (as well as capital) investment in skyscrapers, the task of designing a civic or national landmark is daunting. The glocal skyscraper has become a receptacle for this complex mediation between global and local conditions, becoming a large-scale signifier

fig 3 The Petronas Towers are icons for a national collective imaginary, able to "represent" the ethnically diverse Malaysian population in two towers.

fig 4 The completion of the Petronas Towers signaled a shift in high-rise building activity from North America to Asia.

of identity and community.

Cities around the world, from Kuala Lumpur to Dubai, have experimented with a crop of regionalist-inspired skyscrapers. Drawing explicitly from traditional architectural motifs, often exaggerated in scale and proportion, the designs seek to mediate between a universal building type—the skyscraper—and a local building tradition. [figs 1, 2] The completed buildings are often iconic structures, instantly recognizable. They form powerful, if singular, associations with local building traditions and cultures. The Petronas Buildings in Kuala Lumpur attempt to translate the geometry and profile of a traditional Islamic minaret into a contemporary office building. [figs 3 4] The Jin Mao Building in Shanghai performs a similar mediation, reinterpreting the Chinese multi-tiered pagoda as an office and hotel building. These structures represent progress and modernization, yet still evoke the imagery of tradition and the past. In Taiwan, the Taipei Financial Center is set to capture the title of world's tallest building in 2004. The tower, designed by Taiwanese architect C. Y. Lee, epitomizes the glocal skyscraper—super tall, symbolically charged, and draped with historicist references. [fig 5]

Although transformed by technological advances, one of the skyscraper's most powerful qualities is its symbolism.[2] The skyscraper exploits the symbolic potential of architecture through literal references. As a "text" the skyscrapers are "read" in relationship to a local history of architecture, validating a new form of architecture through a symbolic vocabulary. By explicitly evoking the past, these contemporary and technologically advanced towers create a cultural validity

fig 5 Detail from Taipei Financial Center. The grotesque scale of the applied decorations, meant to recall vernacular building traditions, seem trite and superficial.

through nostalgic means. These thinly applied, culturally specific, architectural features create an appliqué of cultural value that raises difficult questions about the skyscraper as a cultural signifier in a glocal context.

1 Kenneth Frampton, "Towards a Critical Regionalism: Six Points for an Architecture of Resistance," in The Anti-Aesthetic: Essays on Postmodern Culture, Hal Foster, ed., Bay Press, Seattle, 1983, p. 21.

2 Diana Agrest notes, "These attributes of technique, elevator, and scale do not, however, account for an equally critical aspect of the skyscraper's development, namely the problem of meaning." Agrest points to Adolf Loos's 1922 polemical entry for the Chicago Herald Tribune competition—a skyscraper shaped like a giant classica Doric column—as representative of the shift from the column as a functional structural element to an overscaled emblem of a structure whose primary role is symbolic. It articulates a semiotic rift latent in all skyscrapers between the signifying shell and the structural core. Diana I. Agrest, "Architectural Anagrams: The Symbolic Performance of Skyscrapers," in Architecture from Without: Theoretical Framings for a Critical Practice, MIT Press, Cambridge, 1991, p. 79.

TAIPEI FINANCIAL CENTER
C. Y. Lee & Partners, Taipei, 2004

Expected to capture the title of world's tallest building when completed in 2004, the Taipei Financial Center will present a new model for the Asian skyscraper, one explicitly evocative of traditional Chinese architecture. Designed as a segmented shaft of eight outward-sloping segments, the tower resembles a giant glass pagoda. The green-tinted glass cladding is meant to mimic the color of jade. The segments, consisting of eight floors, lean out slightly, creating the distinctly stacked or tiered silhouette.

The tower is dressed in ornamental motifs drawn from traditional Chinese architectural sources. Large-scale ornamental elements and "auspicious emblems" cap each segment. Medallions grace the center of the tower, while decorative features protrude from the corners. An elaborate, stylized spire, 1,667 feet (508 meters) high, will top the structure. Lee's architecture employs botanical as well as traditional architectural themes. Each eight-story segment has been likened to a segment of a bamboo stalk, and the whole project evokes, in the words of the architect, a sense of "petal-like" blooming, giving the tower a sense of "upgrading and fullness," which are important concepts in Chinese culture.

Despite its historicist references, the tower introduces a number of pioneering technological innovations. A giant pendulum suspended from the ninety-second floor acts as a passive mass damper, reducing the building sway at the top of the tower, and counteracting the lateral forces induced by high winds and earthquakes. Other technical innovations include high-speed pressurized elevators that will travel at record-breaking speeds. They will reach the observation deck in just thirty-nine seconds.

Lee's designs strive to give symbolic form to the expression of contemporary "Chineseness." His philosophically-inspired concepts for "bridging past and future" and building in "harmony with nature," tend to manifest themselves in the application of ornamental motifs and symbolic formal translations of building traditions. The combination of traditional Chinese dressing and a contemporary structure creates an unusual and idiosyncratic edifice.

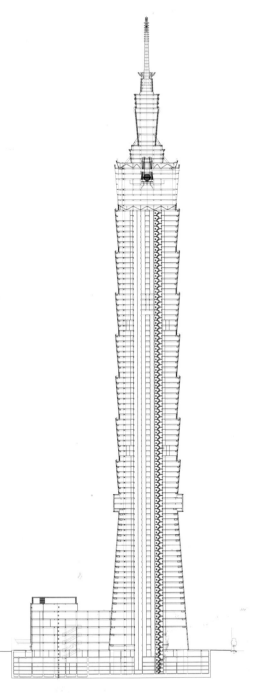

"Bamboo stalk" building section.

Explicit referentiality: Taipei Financial Center evokes a traditional Chinese pagoda through its tiered silhouette.

21

Detail of decorative spire.

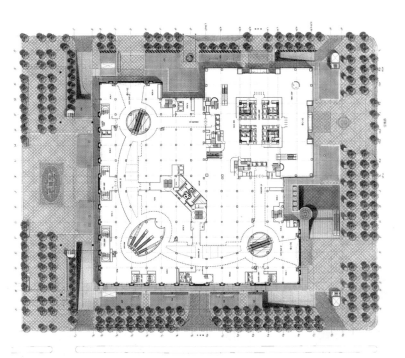

Ground floor plan.

The Taipei Financial Center presents a new model for the Asian skyscraper, one explicitly evocative of traditional Chinese architecture.

JIN MAO TOWER
Skidmore, Owings & Merrill, Shanghai, 1997

This eighty-eight-story building was designed by the Chicago-based firm of Skidmore, Owings & Merrill for Shanghai's Pudong District. One of many skyscrapers built in Shanghai's special economic zone, the building is a showcase project. Declaring the emergence of China as a new economic superpower, Jin Mao Tower's distinct pagodalike profile makes it a new landmark for Shanghai and for China.

The tower's signature profile is made up of a slender shaft of articulated setbacks. As the building rises, it steps back in multiples of eight, evoking the profile of a traditional Chinese pagoda at an exaggerated scale. Clad in glass and stainless steel, the curtain wall is designed with a cage-like system of decorative rails. The heavily articulated facade gives the tower a distinctly ornamented exterior that recalls the decorative carvings on a traditional Chinese structure. The density of external cladding members gives the tower a rich texture, and privileges the external appearance over the interior views. The tower is crowned with a machinelike lotus blossom pinnacle.

Anchored to the ground by a large podium housing retail, conference and exhibition facilities, lobby spaces, and a food court, the building is a veritable city within a city. The tower itself houses offices, a hotel, and retail and conference facilities. Offices occupy the lower fifty floors, and a 555-room hotel occupies the upper half. The hotel is organized around a thirty-story circular atrium, creating a vertiginous interior void in the middle of the shaft. A public observation deck occupies one of the top floors of the tower, providing panoramic views of the urban landscape below.

Attempting to mediate between the local design tradition and a global building type, Jin Mao Tower's heavily ornamented and historically unique form results in an unprecedented cultural monument, appearing simultaneously nostalgic and futuristic. The "Orientalist" architectural vocabulary of Jin Mao Tower raises difficult questions about the design of tall buildings in an Asian context, where references to traditional architecture on contemporary building types result in contradictory cultural iconography on a monumental scale.

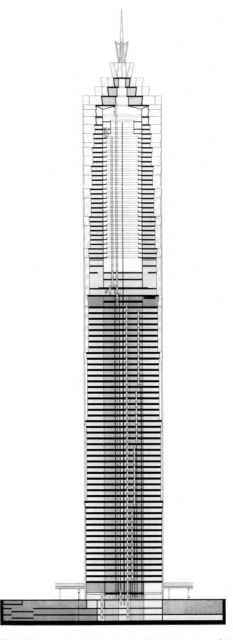

The building section illustrates the diminishing mass of the tower towards the top and the thirty-story hotel atrium.
OPPOSITE: Jin Mao Tower's set-back massing and articulated cladding evoke the traditional Chinese pagoda and vernacular building traditions.

Corridor along the hotel atrium. **OPPOSITE:** View up the atrium.

PETRONAS TOWERS
Cesar Pelli & Associates, Kuala Lumpur, 1997

Declared the tallest buildings in the world when completed
in 1997, these 1,476-foot (450 meter) twin buildings
placed Kuala Lumpur in the global collective consciousness. The twin monuments powerfully embody the
symbolic potential of the skyscraper to declare Malaysia's
arrival on the global stage. Designed by Argentinean-
American architect Cesar Pelli, the buildings seek to give
form to a contemporary Malaysian skyscraper, regional
in derivation and global in aspiration.

Built on the site of the former Selangor Turf Club,
the towers' plans are derived from traditional Islamic
geometric principles, consisting of two rotated squares
in-filled with semicircles. The extruded towers step back
as they rise, giving them a distinctly minaret-like silhouette. A two-story sky bridge links the twin towers at the
forty-second-story sky lobby creating what the designer
has called a "portal to the sky."[1]

Employing traditional motifs and craft traditions, the
architects sought to create linkages to the buildings'
cultural context. The towers are clad in reflective glass
and horizontal stainless-steel sunscreens that filter the
intense tropical sun. Interior spaces are articulated using
traditional patterns and local materials. The paving pattern on the ground floor is derived from "Pandan" weav-
ings and bertam palm wall mattings. The lobby store-
fronts are decorated with hand-carved wooden screens.

The completion of this project, and its claims of
"world's tallest," signaled a symbolic shift in high-rise
building activity, from North America to Asia. The interpretive strategies employed by the architects to "localize"
the design of the building have raised questions concern-
ing "local" or "regional" references in skyscraper designs.
Applied ornaments and references to vernacular traditions seem superficial and nostalgic for a structure of its
stature and global visibility. Appropriate or not, the
Petronas Towers demonstrate the tremendous symbolic
power of the skyscraper, and the explicit role they can
play in establishing a national and cultural identity.

1 Cesar Pelli quoted in *Skyscrapers, An Architectural Type of
Modern Urbanism,* Mario Campi, Birkhauser, Basel, 2000, p. 182.

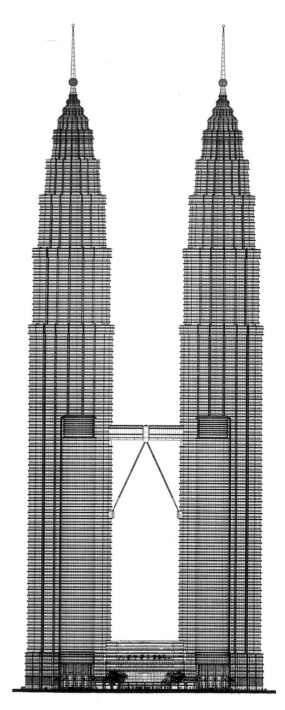

Kuala Lumpur's twin Petronas Towers currently hold the title of "world's tallest" at 1,476 feet. The "sky bridge" links the two towers, creating a new symbolic gateway for the city.
OPPOSITE: Frontal elevation.

Visible from great distances, the decorative twin spires recall the diminishing profile of a traditional Islamic minaret.

high-tech

When Cass Gilbert defined the skyscraper as a "machine that makes the land pay," he was referring to the building's ability to extract value through repetition—repetition of the land on which it sits and repetition of its architectural components. [fig 1]

The skyscraper emerged at the dawn of the industrial revolution, when mass production of standardized parts made these buildings economically possible. It remains the quintessential building type of the twentieth century, and also a celebration of technology and innovation. While all skyscrapers depend on advances in building systems, the "High-Tech" skyscraper celebrates these advances by incorporating structural elements directly into its aesthetic design strategy.

Buildings of the modern period sought to articulate the "true" nature of materials through a kind of structural expressionism. This attitude is most emphatically demonstrated by Mies van der Rohe's design for the Seagram Building. Mies expresses the elements of construction by reducing the steel-frame skyscraper to its bare essentials. Mies then rearticulates the building's systems by applying a structural member, an I-beam, to the exterior as a decorative member. While the building appears to be an honest expression of

fig 1 This partial view of the Chrysler Building photographed by Walker Evans shows the regularity of the structure beneath its masonry cladding.

fig 2 The cross-braced exo-skeleton of the John Hancock building allows the tower to resist lateral loads.

materials and systems, the true structural members are hidden behind the facade, where a steel frame is encased in concrete.

Mies's architectural strip-tease of hidden and exposed structural members highlights the modernist concern with the truthful expression of materials. Truthful expression of materials and systems often has more to do with "expression" than with "truth."

The Hancock Tower and the Sears Tower, both designed by Fazalur Kahn of SOM, are emblematic of exterior structural expression. The tapered shaft and exterior braced-frame tube design of the Hancock Tower articulate the structural roles they play in resisting the lateral forces created by wind and earthquakes. Like the splayed frame of the Eiffel Tower, the wide base of the tower is very stable, and its tapered form expresses a structural diagram. The cross-bracing on the facade allows the tower to distribute loads in three dimensions, making it an inherently stiff structure. *[fig 2]*

The Sears Tower expands on the concept of the perimeter frame, in which a tower's strength is designed into its facade rather than its core, by using a series of "bundled tubes." The building uses nine distinct structural frames, joined together to form a single composite frame. The bundled tube is structurally stronger than all the individual frames alone, and this is expressed in the building's massing by having each distinct frame rise to a different height, creating a setback tower of nine shafts. By placing the structure on the perimeter

fig 3 Hugh Stubbins' Citicorp building in New York.

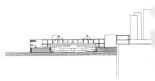

and expressing it so explicitly, the design communicates the structural function of the tower's basic systems.

Hugh Stubbins's Citicorp Tower performs a different kind of structural expression by raising the tower off the street and cantilevering the corners on four megacolumns located at the middle of each face. *[fig 3]* The dramatic effect is increased by the fact that the diagonal bracing structure of the tower is concealed behind a taut skin of an aluminum-and-glass curtain wall. From the outside, one sees a dramatic cantilever, without seeing the structural means that make it possible. In this case, the "High-Tech" approach is revealed through its theatrical architectural effect, rather than through an expressive structural vocabulary.

Sir Norman Foster's Hongkong Shanghai Bank Headquarters extends a language of assemblage to make the expression of the building systems the driving force behind his design. The building suggests a kit of standard parts, assembled in a striking configuration, and implying that what you see is only one of many possible outcomes. In fact, the building is just the opposite, requiring thousands of custom-made, nonstandard parts. *[fig 4]*

"High-Tech" Skyscrapers celebrate the parts over the whole, embracing the process and appearance of assembly. The articulated "kit-of-parts" communicates to the public that the building is the logical outcome of a rational system of construction. They present architecture as inventory and create an aesthetics of assembly.

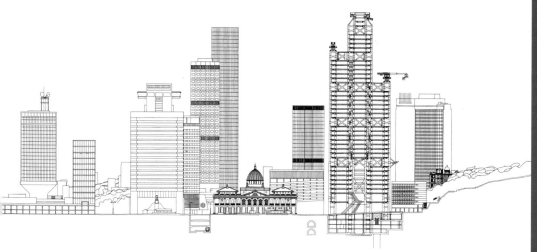

fig 4 Hongkong Shanghai Bank is made up of a megastructural framework with "plugged-in" offices and services.

HONGKONG SHANGHAI BANK HEADQUARTERS
Foster and Partners, Hong Kong, 1985

The de facto cathedral to Hong Kong's commerce, Hongkong Shanghai Bank Headquarters plays a critical symbolic role in the image of the city. Foster's striking steel-and-glass tower stands in sharp contrast to the bank's former headquarters, a monumental granite-clad structure symbolic of the community's financial stability. Foster's design transformed the image of the bank from one of solidity to one of transparency, and in the process, transformed the image of the high-rise office building in Hong Kong.

The building was conceived as a modular system, consisting of megatruss armatures and suspended infill modules. The suspension structure allows for column-free banking halls, while building services, elevator banks, and fire stairs are located on the perimeter. All spaces are organized around the central atrium, which brings light into the core of the building. The resulting building form is a layered assemblage of structural frames that break down the scale of the building and articulated building systems and components.

The building occupies a site of almost spiritual significance in the geomantic atlas determining Hong Kong's fortunes. According to feng shui principles, the flow of energy from the peak to the harbor is critical to the financial well-being of the city. According to geomancers, by raising the tower off the ground and creating a continuous public space at ground

level, the flow of auspicious energy is maintained and channeled into the bank along carefully positioned escalators.

Despite deference to local feng shui beliefs, the language of the tower is developed to express an articulated method of construction. Speed and flexibility are built into the design through the use of modular components and prefabricated parts. Its construction resembled a component assembly plant, rather than a conventional building site. Ironically, the use of prefabricated systems required the custom fabrication of specialized parts rather than the assembly of a kit of off-the-shelf parts. The aesthetic of prefabrication and adaptability is, in fact, highly customized.

The Hongkong Shanghai Bank building epitomizes the high-tech strategy of design through its celebration of building technology, assembly, and methods of construction. Although as Paul Goldberger points out, "While it alludes to a certain rational structure, in truth it is a highly exaggerated, almost baroque expression of modernism's romantic ideals."[1] "Functionalism" here is as much about an expression of function as it is about actual function.

1 Paul Goldberger, "The Skyscraper: Design and Urban Identity at the End of the Twentieth Century," in *Skyscrapers, Higher and Higher*, Caroline Mierop, Norma Editions, Paris, 1995, p. 18.

The north elevation illustrates the suspension structure. **OPPOSITE:** The banking hall, accessed through
the internal atrium via escalators.

The Hongkong Shanghai Bank Headquarters derives its vocabulary from high-tech construction systems used for bridges.

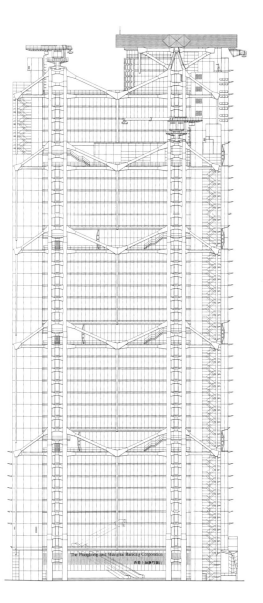

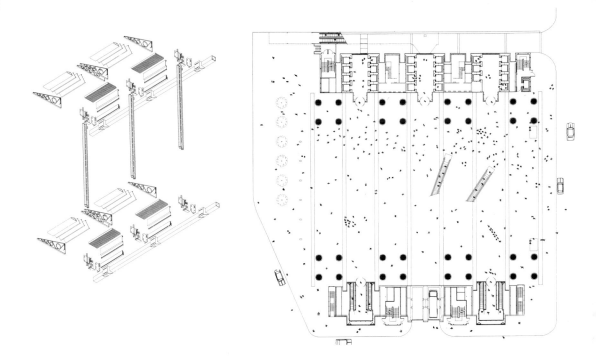

ABOVE LEFT: The inventory of building elements that make up the sun-shading devices. ABOVE RIGHT: Ground-floor plan illustrating the minimal footprint of the tower an the public plaza that runs through it. BELOW: Section through the typical floor illustrates the various building components. OPPOSITE: The internal atrium gathers the banking spaces around it, serving as a vertical community space.

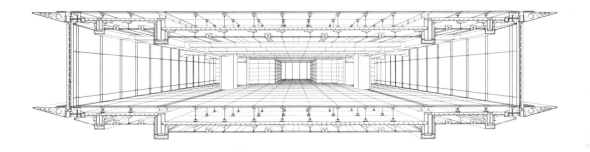

CENTURY TOWER
Foster and Partners, Tokyo, 1991

Often criticized as generic and placeless, the high-rise office building suffers from programmatic banality—office space is homogeneous, repetitive and largely generic. Century Tower proves a rich exception to the norms of the speculative office-building type. Within the tower's articulated shaft are housed a mix of uses and amenities, including a museum, tea house, health club, restaurant, and office space. The expression of the building's diverse parts becomes the central theme of the building.

Century Tower extends concepts first explored in the Hongkong Shanghai Bank. Its facade is articulated as a series of eccentrically braced frames that span across the site to allow for a column-free office space, but also respond to Tokyo's stringent seismic engineering requirements. The tower is broken into two layered blocks joined by an open internal atrium. Each block consists of stacked double-height office floors bridging between structural frames. The atrium connects all the office spaces and creates a sense of community. Building services are housed at the perimeter and are expressed on the facade as stacked vertical elements.

At the foot of the atrium a staircase leads to a museum for the client's collection of Oriental antiquities at basement level. A health club and pool are housed under a curved-glass skylight that slips in under the tower's braced frames. Century Tower celebrates the skyscraper as an assembly of different parts, both structural and programmatic. The various building components are clearly visible from the outside, articulating the building as an architecture of inventory of coexisting programs.

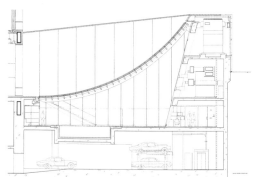

Amenities like the health club and pool on the ground floor make the Century Tower programmatically diverse. **ABOVE:** Section through the curved skylight of the health club.

The tower's layered massing is a function of expressed building systems, structural bays, and perimeter building services.
OPPOSITE: The expression of the building's structural frame gives Century Tower its distinct facade.

BANK OF CHINA
I. M. Pei & Partners, Hong Kong, 1989

The abstract sculptural form of the Bank of China stands out from the thick forest of skyscrapers that make up Hong Kong's eclectic skyline. Designed by the Chinese-American architect I. M. Pei, the design responds to the geographical and cultural context with structural expressiveness and an innovative form.

The building's sculptural form is derived from the correspondence between the tower's volumetric expression and its structural system, a triangulated perimeter tube truss. The tower's volume fills out the triangulated frame in a stepped bundle of prismatic volumes that culminate in a 1,209-foot (369-meter) peak and twin masts. The legibility of the system of support is the source of its dramatic visual strength.

The innovative structural system, designed by engineer Leslie E. Robertson, is a cross-braced perimeter truss. The frame systematically distributes the building's loads and transfers them to four composite corner columns. A fifth column extending through the center of the tower transmits its loads from the tip of the apex down the prow and transfers them out diagonally, leaving the interior of the base of the tower column-free.

The glass-and-metal tower rests on a three-story granite base, which houses the banking hall. A multistory glass atrium connects the banking hall to a skylight at the first setback. The site for the tower is sloped and extremely tight, resulting in access from two different levels. The tower is integrated into a network of abstracted Chinese gardens, which include cascading pools of water and distinctly formed Chinese stones.

According to feng shui, the Chinese geomantic principles that seek to place buildings in a harmonious relationship to their surroundings, the tower's angular form is disruptive to its context. The originally intended X-bracing on the facades was perceived as an aggressive and negative gesture. Although bank officials ignored the warnings of local feng shui masters, Pei chose to conceal the horizontal member, transforming the X into auspicious diamond shapes. The tower is still regarded with reservation by many locals, who claim that its sharp corners direct negative energy towards its neighbors.

Pei's dramatic and structurally expressive design derives its form from an abstract architectural language, employing geometry to interpret the geographical and cultural contexts of the tower. The abstract form of the tower allows for multiple interpretations and associations, making it a multivalent symbol.

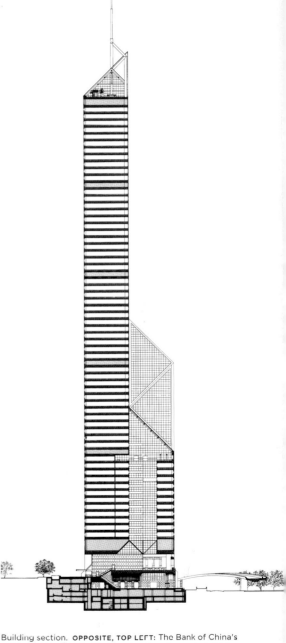

Building section. **OPPOSITE, TOP LEFT:** The Bank of China's polyhedral form and reflective glass facade create kaleidoscopic reflections of the city and the sky. **OPPOSITE, BOTTOM LEFT:** The dome of the Legislative Council chamber stands in sharp contrast to the Bank of China's taut glass facades. **OPPOSITE, RIGHT:** The Bank of China's dramatic presence on the Hong Kong skyline.

WAN XIANG INTERNATIONAL PLAZA
Ingenhoven Overdiek und Partner,
Shanghai, 1995 (designed)

The Wan Xiang International Plaza, designed in 1992
for a site on Nanjing Road in Shanghai, captures the
dynamic economic outlook of the time. Designed by
the German firm Ingenhoven Overdiek und Partner,
the tower was one of the first projects in Shanghai
to be commissioned by a foreign architecture firm.

The complex consists of a fifty-three-story office
tower, and a ten-story retail podium. A glass arcade
cuts diagonally across the site to draw people into
the project from Nanjing Road. The resulting triangular footprint is extruded into the tower's shaft
and set back along sloped facets. Like the Bank of
China Tower in Hong Kong, the faceted geometry
of the tower follows the diagonal structural frame
of the cross-braced structure. The zigzag structure,
designed by Büro Happold, is clearly expressed
through the transparent glass facades.

The project is planned to incorporate an energy-
efficient, naturally ventilated facade, based on
principles developed in Germany on projects like
the RWE office building in Essen, also by
Ingenhoven Overdiek and Partners.

The tower's iconic form, derived from the sculptural expression of the building's structural systems,
gives the building a distinct profile on the city skyline. It also represents an early attempt to introduce
"sustainable design" concepts to the region.

FROM LEFT TO RIGHT: The setback forms and triangulated
structure give the tower its distinct profile; view of the
model illustrates the diagonally braced structure behind the
glass facade; Wan Xiang International Plaza would soar
above Shanghai's bustling streets.

HEARST TOWER
Foster and Partners, New York, 2001 (designed)

The faceted design for a new Hearst Tower stands in sharp contrast to the existing Art Deco Hearst building that it is planned to sit above. Foster's glassy modern design challenges conventional notions of contextualist design and expands the definitions of historic preservation and adaptive reuse.

The original Hearst Building, an historic landmark building designed by Joseph Urban, was only partially completed in 1928. The six-story masonry block with a central courtyard, splayed corners, and theatrical statuary was intended as the base for a tall tower. The original design of the tower remains unknown.

The new tower proposed by Foster will hover above the existing stone base, allowing natural light to enter the podium and maintaining a clean separation between new and old. Foster's philosophy of design for projects that engage historic buildings involves carefully orchestrated contrast. His designs for additions to Berlin's Reichstag and the atrium of the British Museum have been highly acclaimed.

The new Hearst Tower's faceted facade expresses its perimeter-tube structure as a triangulated structural web, or "diagrid." Structurally efficient, the triangulated structure carries its loads diagonally along the perimeter. The chamfered corners articulate the tower's rigorous structural logic and create kaleidoscopic reflections of the city.

In the architect's words, the tower design seeks to "enhance the historic through a carefully orchestrated dialogue with the modern." It employs innovative structural systems that celebrate the techniques of construction and the benefits of contemporary technology, deferring to the original building without mimicking it.

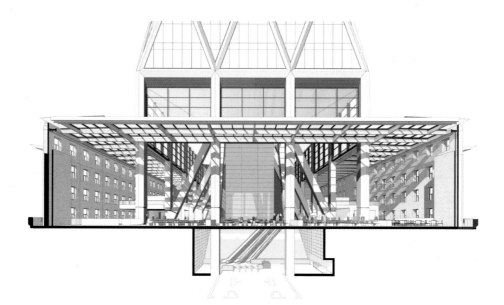

ABOVE: Cutaway perspective illustrates the skylit atrium at the base of the tower. **OPPOSITE, LEFT:** The building section illustrates the structure of the new tower as it engages the existing podium. **OPPOSITE, RIGHT:** Hearst Tower will hover above the 1928 landmarked Art Deco podium, creating a dialogue between the new and the old.

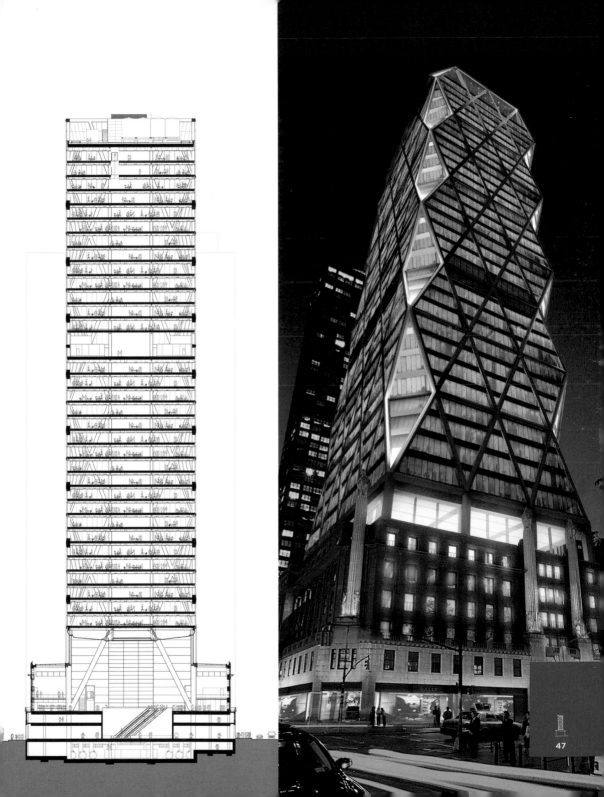

DEBIS HEADQUARTERS
Renzo Piano Building Workshop, Berlin, 1999

The Debis Headquarters forms the centerpiece of
the 1990s redevelopment of Berlin's Potzdamer Platz.
Master-planned by Renzo Piano and Christoph
Kohlbecker, the urban-renewal projects have transformed an area left desolate by the Cold War back
into the vibrant cultural and commercial center that it
was prior to the Second World War.

Piano conceived of the tower as a hybrid building
with a horizontal slab, vertical tower, and open courtyard, carefully combining object and void. The mass of
the building is broken up into a composition of discrete
blocks, organized as bundles of parallel slabs rising to
different heights and culminating in the 350-foot (106-
meter) skyscraper on the southern end of the site. The
atrium is a semi-public central void that invites people
into the building and brings natural light into its center.

Piano's concerns with the expression of a building's
components and means of construction is evident in
the Debis Tower. The building's internal functions, elevators, stairs, office space, and ventilation tower are clearly
articulated on the exterior. The facades are made up
of layers of delicate screens and operable glass panels
filtering out the sun while allowing for natural light and
ventilation. The "opaque" facades are made up of prefabricated terracotta screens that are held in front of an
operable insulated-glass curtain wall.

The "transparent" or "ventilating" facade consists of
a layer of adjustable glass louvers that can be closed
to trap an insulating layer of warmed air, or partially
opened to remove warm air through convection. In
addition to the energy-saving approach to the design
of the facades, the juxtaposition of the terracotta and
glass screens gives the building a visually rich texture.
The warm earth tones recall the solidity of the traditional
urban fabric, while the delicacy and transparency of
the glass louvers reflect light in playful ways, animating
the building, making it appear light and ephemeral.

The redevelopment of the Potsdamer Platz illustrates
a model of development that is able to create a new,
vibrant mixed-use center in a city scarred by destruc-
tion of war. With a building of innovative composition
and careful detailing, the Debis Headquarters project
anchors one end of a redevelopment project celebrated
for being regenerative and reconciliatory, and for heal-
ing the wounds on the city and the psyche.

The internal atrium of Debis Headquarters is a
dramatic public room for events and art exhi-
bitions that brings natural light into the office
spaces. **BELOW:** The facade around the glass-
enclosed stair is a delicate lattice of aluminum
and terracotta extrusions that dematerialize
the building's bulk.

The Debis Headquarters building anchors the southern end of the Potsdamer Platz redevelopment with a long and slender tower articulated as a series of layered surfaces.

The view of the podium prow on Eichhornstrasse.
ABOVE: Pedestrian public spaces along the arcaded base of Debis Headquarters.

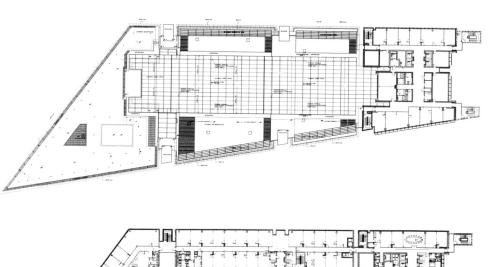

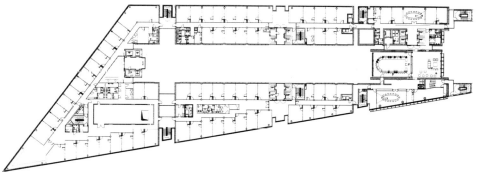

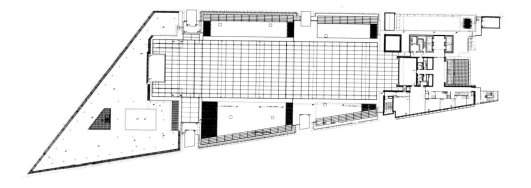

Plans at podium level.

51

The tower model compared to New York landmark structures the Chrysler Building and the Empire State Building.

NEW YORK TIMES HEADQUARTERS
Renzo Piano Building Workshop,
New York, 2000 (designed)

The decision to build a new headquarters for *The New York Times* west of Times Square marks a decisive return by the company that gave Times Square its name. Times Square has been the site of large-scale urban renewal since the mid-1990s, when new legislation and private funds were used to drive out the peep shows and strip clubs in the area, making way for family entertainment. Often referred to as the "Disneyfication" of Times Square, the renewal efforts have transformed the formerly seedy neighborhood into a brightly lit entertainment zone, including multiplex cinemas, Broadway theaters, hotels, retail shops, and a wax museum.

The selection of Renzo Piano as the architect for the fifty-two-story, 748-foot (228 meter) *The New York Times* headquarters was the outcome of an international design competition. Piano's design for the tower as a rectangular volume with a layered facade system stands out for its deceptively simple massing and elegant exterior. The curtain wall is designed to use clear glass behind veil-like layers of thin ceramic cylinders captured in steel frames and held two feet off the glass. Piano's design for *The New York Times* headquarters celebrates the detail while maintaining a disciplined design vocabulary.

Behind the screens, the activities within will be visible through the facade. Glass-enclosed stairs located on the perimeter will animate the facades with the movement of people. On the ground floor, a large internal garden will open the building up to the public, drawing the city into the lobby and providing amenities such as an auditorium, restaurants, and shops.

As their name suggests, the Renzo Piano Building Workshop explores the art and craft of building through their research and building practice. Their varied projects investigate new materials and building systems, refining a language of delicate and diaphanous facades and sculptural building forms. Piano has proposed a glassy tower that celebrates the technology of building systems. The elements of architecture are deployed in the service of achieving a memorable urban effect—a transparent and ephemeral glass tower that invites views and animates the street.

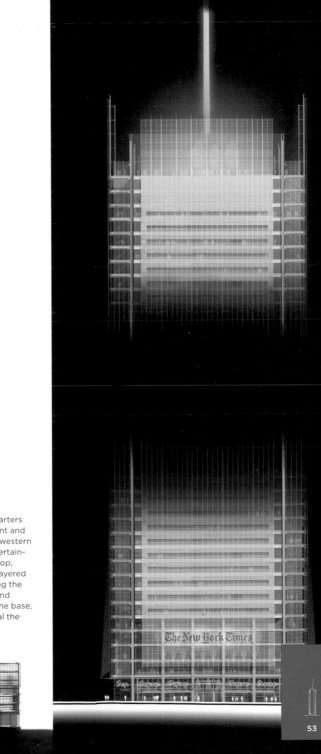

The New York Times headquarters building introduces an elegant and transparent structure to the western end of the Times Square entertainment district. RIGHT: At the top, the design accentuates the layered quality of the facade, allowing the four primary facades to extend beyond the tower mass. At the base, the clear-glass facades reveal the activities within.

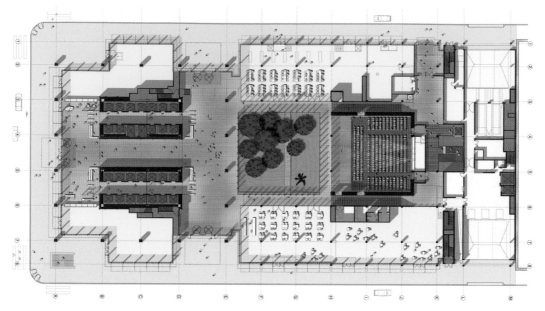

Plan at ground floor level. **BELOW:** Section through the podium illustrating the relationship between the lobby, the garden, and the theater. **OPPOSITE:** The ephemeral effects of the tower facades.

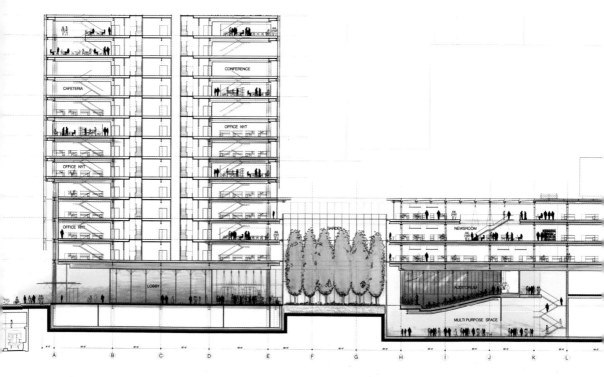

CAFETERIA

CONFERENCE

OFFICE NYT

OFFICE NYT

OFFICE NYT

GARDEN

NEWSROOM

LOBBY

AUDITORIUM

MULTI PURPOSE SPACE

A   B   C   D   E   F   G   H   I   J   K   L

monolithic

The skyscraper is a sublime manifestation of scale. Though designed for human occupancy, the magnitude of repetition that characterizes these buildings exceeds our ability to measure ourselves against them, rendering them unscaleable. Monolithic skyscrapers further exaggerate the effect of scalelessness by employing urban-scale gestures that span their full height. The buildings subsume their programmatic and structural expression in the service of a singular gesture, and in doing so, are placed into the realm of the abstract. These monolithic entities are characterized by platonic solidity, sculptural simplicity, and dramatic form.

Early images of the monolithic skyscraper appear in a number of sources ranging from Frank Lloyd Wright's mile-high skyscraper proposal for Chicago to Hugh Ferriss's series of renderings of early New York skyscrapers. Ferriss captured the essence of the monolithic skyscraper, depicting each mass as if carved from a single colossal block. This abstraction was further articulated by Mies van der Rohe's 1922 project for a glass skyscraper on Friedrichstrasse in Berlin. Rendered as a bold crystalline volume, it captured the aspirations of the "new spirit" in architecture, anticipating by thirty years the first all-glass curtain-wall building. *[fig 1]*

The John Hancock Building in Boston, designed by Henry

fig 1 While Mies van der Rohe's crystalline proposal for an all-glass skyscraper on the Friedrichstrasse in Berlin was never realized it did demonstrate the iconic potential of the monolithic skyscraper.

fig 2 The rhomboidal extrusion of the John Hancock Tower in Boston rejects the articulation of base, middle, and top in favor of a monolithic reflective-glass shaft.

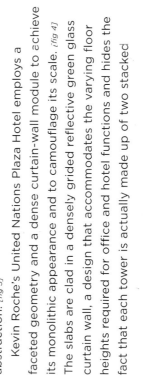

Cobb at I. M. Pei and Partners, captures some of the monolithic elegance of Mies's Friedrichstrasse project. [fig 2]

Many contemporary design practices have returned to the expressive potential of large-scale sculptural gestures. William Pedersen's 333 Wacker Drive creates a curvilinear monolith out of green reflective glass. The building's form, derived from the curve of the river and the grid of the city forms a large-scale urban sculpture. Kohn Pedersen Fox's recent projects for Shanghai and Pusan create urban-scale architectural monoliths, molding mixed programs for offices, apartments, and hotels into singular sculptural forms. In explaining the design strategies for the Shanghai World Financial Center, William Pedersen describes the tower-as-monolith as offering "the dominance of a single melodic line as a point of departure."[1] Currently under construction in Pudong, the Shanghai World Financial Center responds to the dissonant context of Shanghai's rapidly growing business sector with a gesture of powerful restraint, simplicity, and abstraction. [fig 3]

Kevin Roche's United Nations Plaza Hotel employs a faceted geometry and a dense curtain-wall module to achieve its monolithic appearance and to camouflage its scale. [fig 4] The slabs are clad in a densely grided reflective green glass curtain wall, a design that accommodates the varying floor heights required for office and hotel functions and hides the fact that each tower is actually made up of two stacked

fig 3 333 Wacker Drive, William Pedersen's taut-skinned tower on the Chicago River.

fig 4 Kevin Roche's United Nations Plaza Hotel is derived from a similar language of crystalline glass monoliths.

buildings. The masterful play of geometry, modulation, and reflective surfaces results in an astonishing illusion of scalelessness—"a monumental architectural dissolve."[2]

In their introduction to the 1995 exhibition entitled "Monolithic Architecture," Rodolfo Machado and Rodolphe el-Khoury describe the convergence in architectural work that gave its name to their exhibit: "These buildings coincide in their extreme economy and simplicity of overall form and consistency of appearance." These monoliths seek to "maximise the expressive potential of common architectonic configurations by condensing their figurative allusions into one eloquent gesture."[3]

Geometric abstraction and sculptural articulation give monolithic skyscrapers a level of autonomy, allowing them to stand apart from their context, and in some cases recreate it through their iconic presence.

1 William Pedersen, "To Design High," in *Torri e grattacieli (Towers and Skyscrapers)*, l'Arca Plus, l'Arca Edizioni, Milan, 1997, p. 10.

2 Ada Louise Huxtable, quoted in *New York 1960*, Robert A. M. Stern, Thomas Mellins, and David Fishman, Monacelli Press, New York, 1995, p. 636.

3 Rodolfo Machado, Rodolphe el-Khoury, *Monolithic Architecture*, The Heinz Architectural Center, The Carnegie Museum of Art, Prestel-Verlag, Munich, 1995, p. 12.

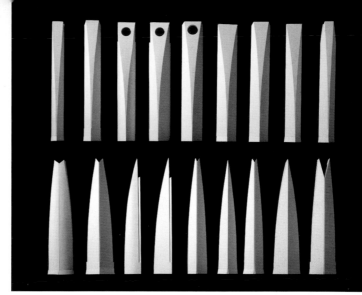

fig 5 A series of studies for Kohn Pedersen Fox's Shanghai World Financial Center reveals a sculptural design process where the mass of the building is carved, as if from a solid block, to reveal the design "embedded" within

LONDON BRIDGE TOWER
Renzo Piano Building Workshop, London, 2002 (designed)

If built, this new 1,016-foot (310 meter) tower proposed for the center of London will be the tallest building in Europe. Designed by Renzo Piano, the Italian architect famous for his sensitive designs for diverse building types, the tower's pyramidal form and great height would make it an immediate iconographic landmark.

The pyramid as a platonic solid has appeared throughout the history of architecture. Monumental structures in Egypt and Mesoamerica employed the pyramid's elemental form to approximate the divine. American architects of the 1930s evoked the pyramid as an ur-form of the set-back skyscraper. The Transamerica Pyramid in San Francisco is the purest embodiment of the skyscraper as a platonic monument. Piano makes references to the spires of London's churches, arguing that the shape of the London Bridge Tower is "generous at the bottom without arrogantly touching the ground and narrow at the top, disappearing in the air like a sixteenth-century pinnacle." Its tapered form is designed to allow natural light to reach the street level.

Planned as an urban catalyst tied to a transportation hub, the development is envisioned as a "vertical town," containing office space, residences, shopping, restaurants, observation decks, a museum, and even facilities for religious observance. The tower's diminishing footprint would accommodate the multiple uses within the tapered shaft. The pyramidal form of the exterior envelope abstracts the setback form of the building's elevator core, smoothing out the stepped profile into a single angular form.

Although the tower has met with preliminary planning approval, it is uncertain if it will be built in its current form. As a proposal, the design has already sparked debate about restrictions on tall buildings in the City of London, where view corridors to St. Paul's cathedral are carefully preserved.

Panorama of London. **BELOW LEFT:** The 1,016-foot London Bridge Tower would be the tallest building in Europe if built. Its great height has sparked debate in London about building-height restrictions. **BELOW RIGHT:** The gently-sloped building section illustrating public spaces within the shaft and at the building's crown.

61

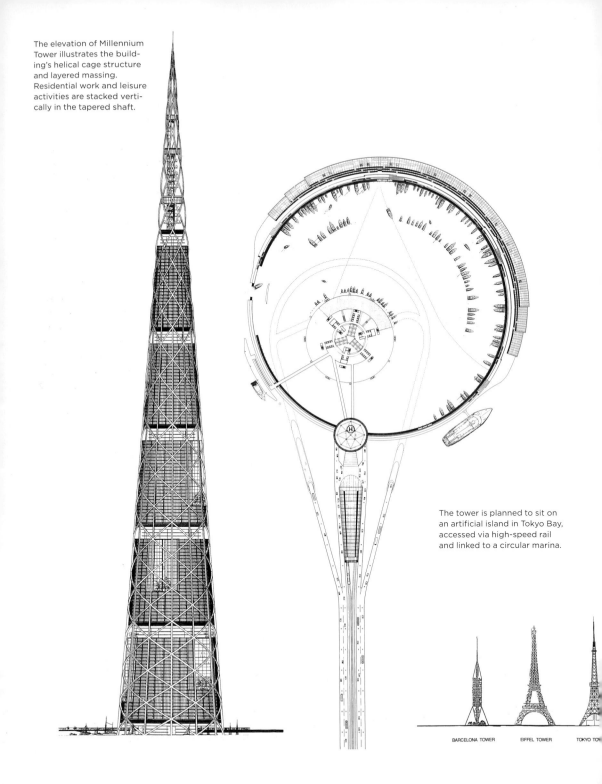

The elevation of Millennium Tower illustrates the building's helical cage structure and layered massing. Residential work and leisure activities are stacked vertically in the tapered shaft.

The tower is planned to sit on an artificial island in Tokyo Bay, accessed via high-speed rail and linked to a circular marina.

BARCELONA TOWER   EIFFEL TOWER   TOKYO TOW

MILLENNIUM TOWER
Foster and Partners, Tokyo, 1989 (designed)

One of the densest cities in the world, Tokyo is a fitting site for Norman Foster's hypothetical Millennium Tower project. The design proposes a fantastical utopian solution to the social challenges of urban expansion and land shortages. The project creates a vertical city that would stand 170 stories, or 2,756 feet (840 meters) tall, and provide for ten million square feet of mixed-use space.

Designed for a site in Tokyo Bay, and connected to other urban centers via high-speed rail systems, the tower forms a high-density urban node within a future urban network. The tower is designed as a self-sustaining vertical city, housing a community of 60,000 people, generating its own energy, and processing its own waste. Office space, light manufacturing, and "clean" industries such as consumer electronics occupy the lower levels. Residential stories are located above, and communications systems as well as wind and solar generators occupy the topmost section.

Vertical circulation is accommodated by express elevators that stop at "sky centers" located at every thirtieth floor. Local elevators and escalators serve the floors in between. The five-story sky centers are designed as the vertical equivalent of the traditional piazza, serving as public hubs containing hotels, retail, and entertainment. Each sky center is articulated with mezzanines, terraces, and gardens.

The tower's conical shape and helical cage structure is a highly efficient structural form, suited for the project's unprecedented height and earthquake-prone location. Its tapering form (similar to the Eiffel Tower's) provides a wide base for stability and a slender and open top, minimizing wind resistance. The tapered form of the Millennium Tower is a pure structural solution in which the building form parallels the force diagram of a vertical cantilever.

The project is a model for high-density living, providing a cluster of urban elements organized around a vertical axis. Departing from modernist schemes for utopian communities that were predicated on a separation of uses in the horizontal plane, Foster's vision for the future of cites combines residential, work, and leisure facilities within the same complex, literally stacked upon one another, minimizing the land-use footprint and maximizing interaction. The project challenges assumptions about the future of cities and envisions high-rise solutions that are "sustainable, efficient, and vibrant vertical communities."

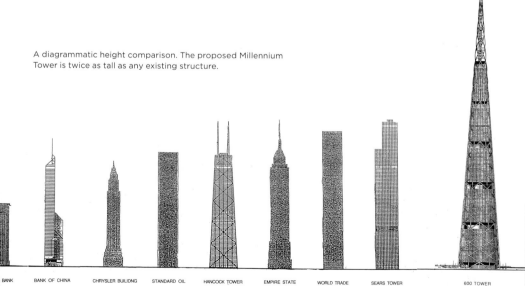

A diagrammatic height comparison. The proposed Millennium Tower is twice as tall as any existing structure.

IG BANK   BANK OF CHINA   CHRYSLER BUILIDNG   STANDARD OIL   HANCOCK TOWER   EMPIRE STATE   WORLD TRADE   SEARS TOWER   600 TOWER

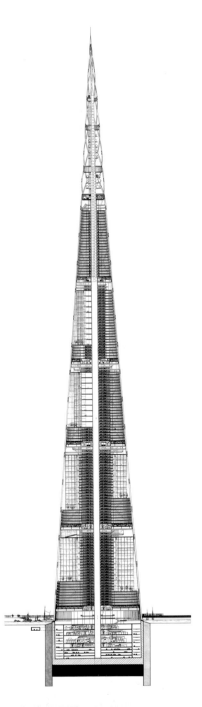

The building section illustrates the open-framework structure and intermittent public spaces between "packages" of floor. **LEFT:** The conical spire would house wind and solar generators.

The proposed Millennium Tower envisions
a new kind of self-sustaining vertical city
as a key component of the urban future.

65

AL FAISALIAH COMPLEX
Foster and Partners, Riyadh, 2000

A distinctly tapered iconic form, the Al Faisaliah Complex in Riyadh is one of Saudi Arabia's first skyscrapers. The mixed-use development combines various program types to form a kind of city-within-a-city; the complex combines office functions, a five-star hotel, a banqueting and conference center, luxury apartments, and a three-story retail mall.

A tower is essentially a column: stoic, iconic, and motionless. However, Foster's design for the Faisaliah Complex, a square-plan, pyramidal tower that tapers along a bowed line to a sharp point, inverts these conventional associations by creating a visual effect of tension. The structural frame of the building is expressed in its corner columns as a series of giant K-braces. The bowed lines of the four main corner columns accentuate the tautness of the curve, creating a visual tension that draws the eye up the entire length of the tower.

The open structure of the tower contains a glass sphere at its top, which houses a restaurant space and an observation deck. At its pinnacle, the tower narrows to a brightly lit lantern and a stainless-steel spire. The building is clad in anodized aluminum sun-shading panels, which minimize glare and give the building a distinct textured appearance.

The tower's pyramidal form evokes a weighty solidity, yet Foster combines an affinity for structural expressiveness with the sculptural elegance that creates a tower of paradoxical lightness.

ABOVE RIGHT: The Al Faisaliah complex combines office, hotel, and retail functions in a mixed-use city-within-a-city. BELOW RIGHT: The view from within the spherical observation deck looks out over Riyadh.

The gently bowed pyramidal form of the Al Faisaliah Complex towers over Riyadh.

30 St. Mary Axe presents a unique profile on the London skyline.

30 ST. MARY AXE HEADQUARTERS
Foster and Partners, London, 2004

This unusually shaped building promises to reinvent the building type through its dramatic form and sophisticated integration of building systems. Located in the heart of London's financial district, the City of London, the building joins a small cluster of tall buildings. The tower sits in a public plaza, reinforcing its sculptural qualities and the notion that it is an object that can be appreciated from all angles.

The tower is circular in plan, widening as it rises from the ground, and then tapering towards its domed apex. In geometric terms the building is a rotational form, the result of spinning a curved line about a single axis. The resultant shape is a bulbous projectile-like structure that defies most skyscraper conventions and conjures up phallic associations.

In his book *Delirious New York*, Rem Koolhaas speculates that the conceptual origins of the skyscraper are to be found in what he calls the "architectural subconscious." He muses that the ideal skyscraper is the result of the desire to be simultaneously a sphere and a needle. "The needle and the globe represent the two extremes of Manhattan's formal vocabulary and describe the outer limits of its architectural choices. The needle is the thinnest, least voluminous structure to mark a location within the Grid. It combines maximum physical impact with a negligible consumption of ground. It is, essentially, a building without an interior. The globe is, mathematically, the form that encloses the maximum interior volume with the least external skin."[1] Koolhaas argues that the history of "Manhattanism" is the dialectic between the two extremes: the needle's desire to attract attention, and the globe's ability to house vast amounts of real estate within its minimal shell. Foster's design for 30 St. Mary Axe evokes some of the same properties, appearing bulbous and axial at the same time.

30 St. Mary Axe utilizes natural ventilation for much of the year, reducing energy consumption and carbon dioxide emissions. The operable curtain wall allows the occupants to enjoy natural light and fresh air, as well as an increased connection to the outdoors. The envelope is comprised of two layers of glass and a ventilated cavity. Fresh air is drawn through the building envelope, and is ventilated by natural convection through light wells that spiral up the building perimeter.

When completed in 2004, the building will be the first environmentally progressive tall building in London. In the architect's words, "The building is radical—technically, architecturally, socially, and spatially." The construction of the project signals a shifting of attitudes towards high-rise buildings in the City of London, and a shifting paradigm in terms of what a skyscraper can be and what it wants to be.

1 Rem Koolhaas, *Delirious New York,* The Monacelli Press, New York, 1994, p. 27.

30 St. Mary Axe combines dramatic form and progressive technologies to reconceive the skyscraper building type.

TORRE AGBAR
Jean Nouvel, Barcelona, 2003

Jean Nouvel's design for the Torre Agbar in Barcelona shares many of the qualities of Norman Foster's 30 St. Mary Axe project. Its explicitly bulbous form appears to be a literalization of the skyscraper as phallus. At 466 feet (142 meters), the tower will be among the tallest structures in Barcelona.

Nouvel claims that the form is a desire to transform the solidity of the skyscraper into the ephemerality of a tower of water—a building as fountain. "This tower reads as a fluid mass which has perforated the ground, a geyser under constantly regulated pressure."[1] This theory evokes Thomas van Leeuwen's claim that early Manhattan skyscrapers were, in fact, inspired by frozen fountains.[2]

The tower consists of an elliptical footprint within an elliptical envelope. An offset core floats asymmetrically within the plan, and perimeter elevator banks are grouped along the eastern elevation. Towards the top, the inner ellipse sets back from the exterior envelope, creating a terraced structure within a domelike shell.

The facade is designed to create the ephemeral effects of a liquid, with reflections and undulations. The facade design is a random pattern of repetitive modules that create a shimmering effect and fluid reflections: "smooth, continuous but vibrant and transparent as well, because the material may be read in depth as colored and uncertain, luminous and shaded."

Nouvel's bold gestural design for Barcelona is in keeping with his determination to remain aggressively avant-garde. His buildings do not share a single formal language; instead, they are characterized by an audacity that perpetually challenges the limits of convention.

1 *Next: 8th International Architecture Exhibition*, La Biennale di Venezia, Rizzoli Publications, Venice, 2002, p. 218.

2 Thomas van Leeuwen, *The Skyward Trend of Thought: The Metaphysics of the American Skyscraper*, MIT Press, Cambridge, 1988, p. 132.

Unfolded elevation of curtain-wall system of random patterns of glass that give the tower its luminous appearance.

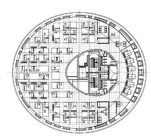

Typical tower plan.

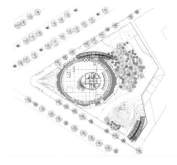

Ground floor plan.

An architectural geyser, Torre Agbar evokes a column of water as an ephemeral monument.

GEOMETRY OF TOWER

The Pudong district of Shanghai has been transformed from a low-density neighborhood opposite Shanghai's Bund to a city of towers, three of them planned to be taller than eighty stories.
LEFT: Floor plan matrix showing the variation in form as one moves up the tower.

SHANGHAI WORLD FINANCIAL CENTER
Kohn Pedersen Fox Associates, Shanghai, 2008

The Pudong district in Shanghai is a showcase special
economic zone, symbolizing China's emergence as a
global economic superpower. Pudong has recently experi-
enced an explosive building boom, making it the largest
building site in the history of the world. When completed,
the Shanghai World Financial Center will become the
centerpiece of the district and will capture the title of
the tallest building in the world. For architect William
Pedersen, the design of the Shanghai World Financial
Center addresses the complexities of the building's
context through a gesture of "heightened simplicity,"
responding through "geometry in its purest form."[1]

The primary form of the tower is an intersection of a
square extrusion and two arcs, which taper to a single
diagonal line at the apex. The gradual transformation
corresponds to large office floorplates at the base, and
narrow, oblong hotel floorplates at the top. The top is
pierced by a circular opening, which houses an observation deck and helps to relieve wind pressure. According
to Pedersen, "the tall building must relate the earth and
the sky." The square plan at the base and the circular
opening at the top make abstract associations to Chinese
cosmology, where the earth is understood as square and
the heavens represented by a circle. This abstract dialogue between two primary forms allows for multiple
interpretations. Some interpreted the "window to the sky"
as a Chinese moon-gate, others as the rising sun in the
Japanese flag (the developer is Japanese).

The continuous transformation of the tower's form
makes each floorplate entirely unique, resulting in a monolithic form of immense volumetric simplicity and great
planimetric complexity. The singular gesture of its sculptural form masks the tower's multiple functions. Equally
proportioned horizontal bands of reflective glass give the
tower a scaleless quality.

In describing the design strategies for the Shanghai
World Financial Center, Pedersen explains how the monolithic tower offers "the potential to generate a symbolic
abstractness which could resonate with the place."[2]

1 William Pedersen, "To Design High," in *Torri e grattacieli (Towers
and Skyscrapers)*, l'Arca Plus, l'Arca Edizioni, Milan, 1997, p. 12.

2 Ibid.

Kowloon Station Tower groups with the International Finance Center 2 to create Hong Kong's Harbor Gateway.

KOWLOON STATION TOWER
Kohn Pedersen Fox Associates, Hong Kong, 2007

Planned for a site on west Kowloon across the harbor from Hong Kong Island, this tower is part of a large development project, including a high-speed rail link between the city and the airport. When completed, the 108-story Kowloon Station Tower will pair with the 88-story International Finance Center Tower on the Hong Kong Island side to form the "harbor gateway."

Kowloon Station Tower is a sculpted, square extrusion that flares out at the base and tapers inward toward the top. At the base, the cladding peels away to create canopies on three sides and an extended skylit atrium on the fourth. At the top, the four primary facades are extended past the roof, creating a glass crown. The tapering form corresponds to the need for smaller floor plates for a hotel at the top, and deeper floor plates for office use below. The hotel is organized around a circular atrium with restaurants and a bar occupying the 108th floor under the glass-crowned skylight space.

The tower is clad in a shingled skin of reflective glass that hides the different functions within and gives the tower a solid, sculpted quality. The shingled facade design consists of offset curtain-wall units, corresponding to each floor, that give the tower a distinct texture.

The Kowloon Station Tower is representative of a pattern of high-density, mixed-use development in Hong Kong planned around infrastructural nodes. Each node is a semiautonomous city-within-a-city accessed by rail, anchored by a multilevel retail mall, and surmounted by residential and office towers. The planning and design of these high-density nodal developments allow urban centers to grow in controlled patterns, making Hong Kong a case study for future cities.

The massive tower, which will capture the title of world's tallest when completed in 2007, conceals its enormous volume through careful sculpting and articulation. Reentrant corners splayed at the top and bottom transform the shaft into an abstract sculpture.

TOUR EDF
Pei Cobb Freed and Partners, Paris, 2001

La Défense business district outside of Paris extends the city's historic axis from the Louvre in the heart of Paris, down the Champs Elysées to the new Grand Arche. By encouraging high-rise development outside the city, but along the city's monumental axis, La Défense district accommodates urban growth and preserves the symbolic alignment that has served as Paris's historic ordering system. The buildings around La Défense are a mixture of heroic monuments and banal office blocks, and the recently completed Tour EDF, designed by Pei Cobb Freed and Partners, is a dramatic new addition to the district along the elevated pedestrian mall, or "dalle."

The forty-one-story tower is designed as a bowed figure of sculptural simplicity. Eye-shaped in plan, the tower is extruded vertically, with a carved-out channel forming a concave hollow in the prow. The entrance to the tower is located at the prow, under a saucerlike canopy that is lodged into the recess.

The building's taut curtain wall gives the tower a sleek, streamlined appearance. Unlike the architectural firm's other monolithic towers—the Hancock Building in Boston, for example—the Tour EDF expresses the floors of the tower with horizontal bands of metal spandrel panels. The ribbonlike panels trace the contours of its sculpted form, making it legible from a distance.

The tower's distinctive form is the result of a geometrically abstract, sculptural handling of its mass. As with other monolithic towers, it appears to be carved from a single solid, and in this case, stratified block.

Tour EDF extends the city's historic axis from the Louvre in the heart of Paris, down the Champs Elysées to the new Grand Arche. **OPPOSITE:** Tour EDF's taut skin and sculptural form creates a sleek new presence along Paris's La Défense district.

SONY CENTER
Murphy/Jahn, Berlin, 2000

The Sony Center, located at the site of historic Potsdamer Platz, is part of the reconstruction of Berlin following German reunification. A mixed-use, mixed-scale project, the complex includes office space, cinemas, and a museum, as well as restaurants and outdoor cafes. The project, which occupies an irregularly shaped city block, creates a complex of buildings surrounding an elliptical covered plaza. Together the buildings define a new kind of public space—permeable and open to the public, yet shielded from the elements by a large canopy structure and saturated with the elements of a new media lifestyle.

The reconstruction and redevelopment of Potsdamer Platz has created a new entertainment center in the void left by the removal of the Berlin Wall. As part of the reconstruction of Berlin, the project employs a strategy of collage, incorporating fragments of existing historical buildings. The historical elements are reprogrammed and reused, without recreating their historic styles.

The tower portion of the development emerges as a semicircular prow to the triangular site. Its convex massing reverses the concave enclosure of the interior plaza. Clad entirely in glass, the tower's sculptural form appears diffuse at its edges, where facades extend beyond the building mass, seeming to dissolve against the sky. Jahn uses external vertical glass mullions to span between floors, exploiting the natural color and optical characteristics of the glass, making the building shift from clear to green, depending on the viewing angle. Taking advantage of new high-performance glass, Jahn accomplishes a crystalline architecture that was anticipated by Mies van der Rohe, but considered unbuildable in his day.

Jahn's approach to technology is exemplified by his term "archineering" which calls for "an innovative interdisciplinary exploration of the applied art of engineering."[1] Throughout the Sony Center, Jahn has been able to apply his principles on an urban scale, creating a high-tech complex that blurs the boundaries of public and private space, civic amenity and corporate enclave. In the words of the architects, "Sony Center is a Kulturforum for the millennium . . . an urban forum for a changing cultural and social interaction of our time."[2]

1 Helmut Jahn, Werner Sobek, *Archi-neering*, Hatje Cantz Verlag, Ostfildern, 1999, p. 12.

2 Ibid.

The clear glass façade utilizes exterior glass mullions that create dramatic optical effects. **OPPOSITE, TOP:** The tower's luminous nighttime presence. **OPPOSITE, BOTTOM:** The exterior glass mullions of the clear glass facade.

AURORA PLACE
Renzo Piano Building Workshop, Sydney, 2000

The design of Aurora Place draws a relationship between its curved facades and the iconic sculptural form of the Sydney Opera House. This gestural building appears to be less a volume than an organic composition of surfaces. The building volume is nested in the interstitial spaces between the two curved, enveloping surfaces.

The tower facades are taut clear-glass panels treated with a silkscreened pattern that cuts down on solar heat gain and gives the tower a diaphanous white appearance. The glass facades extend beyond the building volume, blurring the extent of its mass, and giving the tower a sense of lightness. Operable windows allow for natural ventilation and provide occupants with a connection to the outside environment. The incorporation of natural light and ventilation makes the building both energy-efficient and a hospitable place to work.

The mixed-use project consists of a 44-story, 656-foot (200 meter) tall office tower and a 17-story residential podium. The complex is stepped towards the botanical garden, respecting the light angle so as not to cast shadows over the garden. A small public plaza is located between the two buildings, sheltered by a delicate web-like glass canopy. Within the tower, internal atrium spaces and winter gardens create semipublic informal gathering spaces, making the tower a "vertical village."

Sensitive to the buildings in its historic context, the lobby is clad in a terracotta panel system that complements the local sandstone. Piano's contextualism is not simply one of imitation, but rather a subtle and interpretive response. Aurora Place manifests Piano's interest in making a structure that is sculpturally bold and contextually sensitive— a "naturally ventilated, low-energy building that is also a vibrant social mechanism."[1]

1 Peter Buchanan, *Renzo Piano Building Workshop*, Volume Four, Phaidon, London, 2000, p. 227.

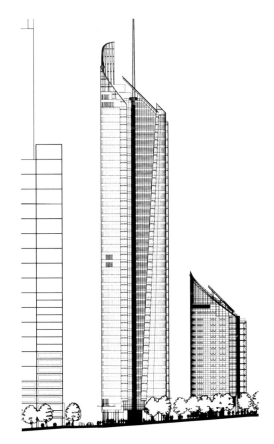

The curvilinear forms of Aurora Place gesture to Sydney's iconic landmark the Opera House. **ABOVE:** The sloped profiles of Aurora Place give the tower a dramatic sail-like presence while minimizing its presence on Sydney's Botanical Gardens across the street.

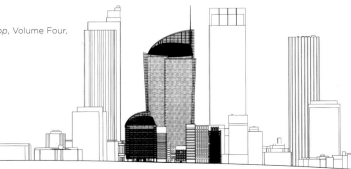

LEFT: Aurora Place is made up of curving glass surfaces that embrace the tower volume within, evoking nautical as well as botanical associations. **RIGHT:** Aurora Place with Sydney's Botanical Garden's beyond.

DAEWOO TOWER 88
Kohn Pedersen Fox Associates, Pusan, 1997 (designed)

The elegant Daewoo Tower 88 exemplifies the subtractive sculptural approach for the design of a monolithic skyscraper. The mixed-use complex was designed for a waterfront site in Pusan, Korea, as part of the larger master plan development to be built on landfill in Suyoung Bay. The project engages its context—cultural as well as geographical—through a sculptural language and interpretive geometry.

The form of Daewoo Tower 88 is derived from an eye-shaped extrusion that is intersected by two offset, curved, cutting planes, resulting in a dramatic tapered form that evolves as it rises. The dominant longitudinal axis of this form implies a connection between the sea and the mountains. The project relates to its context through an abstract language that attempts to symbolically incorporate characteristics meaningful to Korean culture, but is not limited to pictorial or image-based historical precedents.

The tower houses offices, a hotel, and serviced apartments. Functionally, the building's larger lower levels provide flexible office space, while the smaller upper floors, hollowed by a north-facing atrium, house hotel and apartment functions. A stone base and an eye-shaped reflecting pool ground the tower. The podium, housing a concert hall, hotel ballroom and banquet facilities, retail space, and a museum, are composed as a collection of forms that seem to spiral off of the tower's curved form.

Although it is unlikely to be built, the Daewoo Tower 88 exemplifies the sculptural design strategies proposed by William Pedersen. The highly abstract language of geometrically derived forms seeks to create a bold sculptural building that resonates with aspects of the local culture. The curve of a brushstroke or the gesture in traditional Korean dance is evoked through the gesture of the tower. The abstract geometrical language creates a new landmark that invites multiple associations.

Daewoo Tower 88 was planned as a focal point for a new neighborhood built on landfill in Pusan's Suyoung Bay, anchoring a new precinct that combines office, residential, retail, and recreational uses.

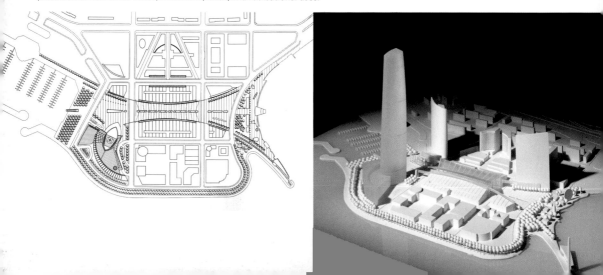

The sail-like forms of the Daewoo Tower 88 taper as they rise.

Daewoo Tower 88 consists of a mix of uses. Office space, hotel rooms, and serviced apartments are stacked within a single tapered shaft.

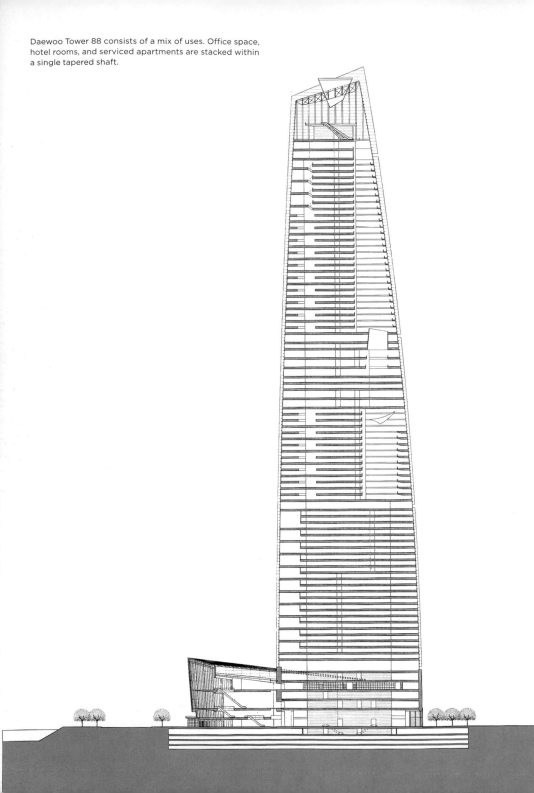

At the base of the tower, a conical museum houses modern sculpture. Brancusi's *Bird in Flight* sculpture served as inspiration for the tower's form.

NATIONAL BANK OF DUBAI
Carlos Ott and Norr Limited, Dubai, 1998

The striking bronze-colored National Bank of Dubai is one of several new buildings in Dubai that signal a desire to shape the image of the city as one of a sophisticated commercial center. Located along the busy waterfront, the facade reflects both the sky and the water in its curved mirror. The reflection, like a fun-house mirror, distorts the image, capturing a broad expanse of sky and water, giving the building an ephemeral appearance.

The curved facade is inspired by the sails of the local ships that ply the river. The building massing suggests a two-part composition. The supporting core, clad in stone, houses the building-services cores. The curved-glass volume seems suspended from the stone volume, emphasizing its sail-like lightness. The curved volume is terminated with vertically articulated fins.

Making up the building's base is a retail podium housing shops and restaurants. The language of convex bows and arcs informs the expression of the podium roof, which appears to hover over the building base.

The National Bank of Dubai building is a mirror for Dubai, reflecting an image of the city as it may want to be seen—modern, progressive, and business-friendly. As with many buildings of this type, the National Bank of Dubai condenses, in its reflective facades, the aspirations of its citizens and builders.

Architect's sketch of the National Bank of Dubai.

The National Bank of Dubai's sail-like form evokes the imagery of the merchant ships that established Dubai as a center of trade.

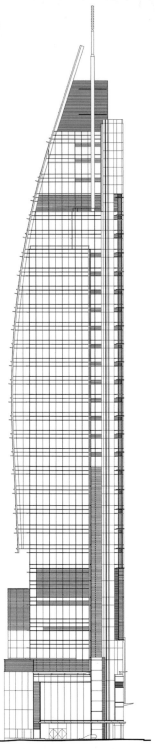

ONE PEKING ROAD
Rocco Design Limited, Hong Kong, 2003

The design for One Peking Road in Hong Kong presents a sculptural new addition to the Kowloon skyline. Its gently bowed facade extends over its orthogonal support, culminating in a thin edge. Viewed from the Hong Kong island side, the building towers above its low-rise neighbors and gestures towards the harbor.

Building heights on the Kowloon side of the harbor have historically been capped to allow airplanes to land at the former airport. Now that the airport has moved to Lantau, the height cap has been lifted, and Kowloon has seen a surge in building activity, with new buildings towering over the existing structures.

The cladding design reinforces the distinct character of the curved and orthogonal volumes. Heavily articulated horizontal shades screen out the intense sun, allowing the glazing to be more transparent. The curved facade culminates in a support structure for south-facing photovoltaic panels. The cladding on the orthogonal volume incorporates a triple-glazed ventilated cavity wall that acts as a thermal buffer. It is the first instance of a double-skin cavity curtain wall in Hong Kong.

In a city known for its mirrored urbanscape, the bold sculptural form and the clear glass at One Peking Road make it a distinctive new landmark. The tower's use of a sophisticated cladding system signals an increased concern for the integration of environmental controls and a new level of design sophistication.

One Peking Road's gently bowed façade extends over the bar-shaped tower and gestures back towards Hong Kong's Victoria Harbor.

KINGDOM CENTER
Ellerbe Becket, Riyadh, 2003

The boldly sculptural Kingdom Center forms a dramatic new focal point on Riyadh's skyline. At a height of 984 feet (300 meters) it will be visible from virtually anywhere in the city. Its signature parabolic crown and streamlined massing makes it a futuristic icon.

The client, Prince Alwaleed, commissioned the building to be a globally recognized icon of Riyadh and Saudi Arabia, just as the Eiffel Tower is a symbol for Paris and France. The design brief required a "simple, strong, monolithic, symmetrical structure." The architects produced a design of fluid curves and clean lines to create the new sculpted landmark.

The entire complex is made up of convex and concave arcs. The tower's footprint is an almond-shaped extrusion with reentrant corners. The podium facilities at its base are organized as crescent-shaped bars that converge on the tower. The catenary curve at the top creates the dynamic image for the project, but is also a form that is found in nature and has a distinct structural logic: it is the arc assumed by an unloaded suspension structure.

The mixed-use Kingdom Center will include a five-star Four Seasons Hotel, a luxury three-level retail mall, office space, the headquarters of a large Saudi Arabian bank, luxury condominiums and apartments, a wedding/conference center, and a sports club. The bridge across the top houses an observation deck.

The multiple functions housed in the tower are enclosed in a single sleek glass envelope. The reflective glass curtain wall masks the activities within and creates the appearance of a taut monolithic form.

The design creates a new landmark for Riyadh, one that is contemporary, abstract, and monumental. It is a boldly sculptural, forward-looking symbol that may, like the Eiffel Tower, one day become fused with the city and nation that it represents.

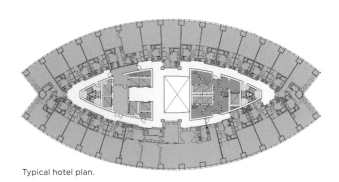

Typical hotel plan.

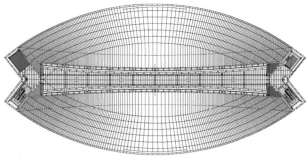

Observation-deck plan.

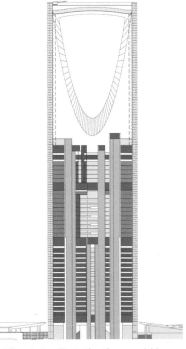

Building section illustrating the occupiable space in the shaft and the hollow areas around the parabolic opening.

ESPIRITO SANTO PLAZA
Kohn Pedersen Fox Associates, Miami, 2003

The new Esprito Santo tower creates a striking corporate headquarters for the bank through a highly sculptural, geometrical composition. Its dramatic parabolic form is the result of the intersection of a cylinder and a sloped bar. The cylinder is subtracted from the wedge, revealing an oblique figure of the gentle curve.

The tower houses office functions at the base, and hotel and serviced apartments towards the top. A multistory atrium at the top of the slab organizes the hotel functions and creates an elevated garden overlooking the city. The tower's multiple functions are not expressed on the facade; instead they are subsumed by the singular swooping gesture. The exterior expression of a singular whole supercedes the articulation of individual interior elements.

Elements within the composition are articulated through the use of cladding textures, analogous to the grain in a block of wood. The carved slab at the front is clad in a uniform horizontal curtain wall. The rear volume is clad in a vertically articulated fabric. A horizontally striated podium-parking structure sits behind the tower. Its connection to the tower is expressed through the gesture of interlocking masses.

The whole complex shares a uniform language of subtractive sculpture, allowing volumes to be carved, slipped, and interlocked. The abstract treatment of forms allows each of the parts to be articulated, revealing the latent geometry of the arched parabola and creating a multistory geometric sculpture.

...uito Santiago... a striking urban icon by sculpting ...he building mass to reveal the latent geometry of the ...rched parabola.

Panorama of Manhattan's midtown skyline.
The Trump World Tower appears with its
self-described precedent, the iconic modernist
slab of the United Nations Secretariat Building.

TRUMP WORLD TOWER
Costas Kondylis & Partners, New York, 2001

Built across the street from the United Nations headquarters, the Trump Tower rises straight up in a slender shaft that defies our expectations of structural
viability. Its simple form, slender proportions, and
minimal facade treatment make it an enigmatic sculptural monolith. The tower is the newest, and tallest,
skyscraper in a constellation of buildings each named
Trump Tower.

The tower houses luxury apartments of varying
sizes, from one to six bedrooms, and addresses the
demand for luxurious, loftlike spaces that can be flexi-
bly planned. Amenities include a lavishly decorated
lobby, a private garden, a private wine cellar, valet
parking, a four-star restaurant on the ground floor,
and a health club with a sixty-foot lap pool.

Its small rectangular site dictates the form of the
tower, and its footprint is extruded straight up 860
feet (262 meters). Making reference to International
Style landmarks like the United Nations building
across the street, the tower is a singular orthogonal
volume without setbacks, which is clad in an unarticulated curtain wall—Trump's signature bronze glass—
and structural silicone glazing. Architect Costas
Kondylis states, "It was designed to look like a slab
cut out of one big piece of glass."[1]

The slenderness of the tower combined with the

requirement that the apartment layouts be flexible
posed challenges to the structure of the building.
The substantial wind and seismic design loads and
the slenderness ratio of 11:1 make it difficult to achieve
the necessary stiffness without intrusive structural
members. High-strength concrete and careful planning
of structural members achieved the required structural
performance.

A controversial project, the tower exploits New York
City's zoning laws and air-rights transfers to achieve
its unprecedented proportions. Unused allowable
building height was purchased from adjacent properties and consolidated on this site. Residents in neigh-
boring buildings, who claimed that the new structure
would block their views, contested the planning of the
project. They were unsuccessful in stopping construction, but the city's zoning laws have since changed,
making the tower the last of its kind.

Developer Donald Trump, who once declared,
"I know what rich people want," has created a signature brand of luxury residential towers that are austere
on the exterior and lavishly decorated on the interior.
For this tower, luxury is in the finishes, not the form.

1 Costas Kondylis quoted in "Now Built, Trump World Tower
Wins Over Critics," by Jerome Belson, *ABO Developments*,
Fall 2002, New York, p. 29.

A relentlessly rectilinear extrusion, the Trump World Tower rises 860 feet in a single unarticulated volume.

The monolithic glass facade, designed to look like the whole shaft was carved from one big piece of glass.

Trump World Tower framed by the United Nations Secretariat Building.

Lille's train station is one part of a master plan designed by Rem Koolhaas.

CREDIT LYONNAIS
Christian de Portzamparc, Lille, 1995

This unusual L-shaped tower is part of the redevelopment of the city of Lille, France, which has found itself at the crossroads of a major regional redevelopment as a result of new high-speed rail links. Halfway between London and Paris, the city has reinvented itself as an infrastructure hub and a shopping and conference center.

The master plan, designed by Rem Koolhaas of OMA, claims that Lille "will become the center of gravity for the virtual community of fifty million Western Europeans who will live within a one-hour traveling distance."[1] As part of the master plan, the city center has been transformed by a new train station, shopping mall, and convention center. The office towers house the new population of businesses relocating to this new, artificial center—a trans-European office park.

The sculpted mass of the Crédit Lyonnais tower is simultaneously a bridge and a tower, spanning the new railway station. Its L-shaped profile houses conference facilities in the bridge and office space in its shaft. Its facades, consisting of randomly distributed patterns of trapezoid-shaped punched-out windows, are undifferentiated from the horizontal bridge to the vertical shaft. The sculptural flare at the top and the uniform treatment of the facades make the tower appear as a single monolithic volume.

The city of Lille is a geographic anomaly: an infrastructural aberration located at the crossroads of a new technology—the high-speed TGV trains. As theorized by Koolhaas, the city and its cluster of stocky skyscrapers have become the site for European experimentations with urban density.

1 Rem Koolhaas and Bruce Mau, *S,M,L,XL,* The Monacelli Press, New York, 1996, p. 1158.

The Credit Lyonnais building is simultaneously a tower and a bridge, spanning the rail tracks with a podium that houses conference facilities.

MAX REINHARDT HAUS
Eisenman Architects, Berlin, 1992 (designed)

Peter Eisenman's provocative design for the Max Reinhardt Haus in Berlin seeks to challenge conventional notions of architecture, and specifically of the skyscraper. Based on the concept of a Möbius strip—a two-dimensional ribbon that twists to form a continuous loop with no distinct inside or outside—the tower is ambiguous as to whether it is one building or two, and also as to where it begins and ends. Eisenman's design places complexity and heterogeneity over purity and order.

Named for the famous German theatrical entrepreneur, the Max Reinhardt Haus is designed to house a broad mix of entertainment programs: a media center, spa and fitness facilities, an auditorium, and several restaurants, as well as office and hotel space. The project seeks to gather up the urban landscape around it and fold it into the building through its many facets. It is contextual by reflecting and incorporating the disjunctions of the surrounding urban fabric. In the words of the architect, "This 'folded' state will result from a gathering or bundling of the urban dimensions of Berlin to simulate in one building the tendential density of the metropolis."[1]

Designed at a time when the computer was beginning to have an impact on the process of architectural design, the project exhibits a new geometric complexity attributed to the computer software. The intersection of architectural theory and new computational software manifests itself in Eisenman's work, creating conditions of new geometric possibilities.

Eisenman's design comments on the monumentality of architecture as built form and as a discourse. His Möbius tower denies the skyscraper the ability to be seen as a singular, pure, or autonomous object. Its heterogenous massing is articulated with a homogenous cladding, emphasizing the tower's monolithic solidity, and reinforcing the tower's inherent monumentality. Through the design of the Max Reinhardt Haus, Eisenman has created new monumentality, one driven by complexity and computation.

1 Peter Eisenman, *El Croquis 83*, Alejandro Zaera-Polo, ed., Madrid, 1997, p. 114.

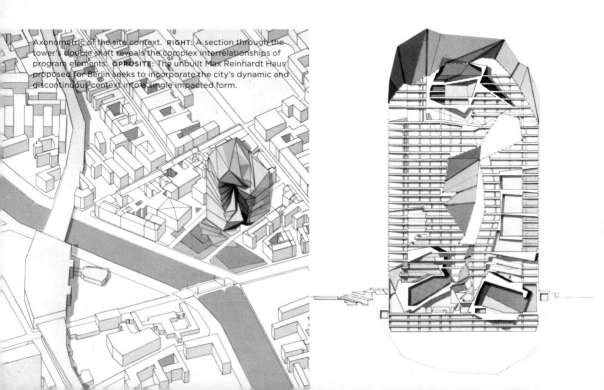

Axonometric of the site context. **RIGHT:** A section through the tower's double shaft reveals the complex interrelationships of program elements. **OPPOSITE:** The unbuilt Max Reinhardt Haus proposed for Berlin seeks to incorporate the city's dynamic and discontinuous context into a single impacted form.

CCTV HEADQUARTERS
Office for Metropolitan Architecture, Beijing, 2008

The new CCTV headquarters designed by Rem Koolhaas of OMA will provide an opportunity for the multidisciplinary firm to test out their urban and architectural theories in built form. Koolhaas's extensive research on the skyscraper, published in *Delirious New York* and *S,M,L,XL,* and more recently in *The Great Leap Forward,* has positioned him as a highly polemical designer and practitioner.

The winning proposal from an international competition, the OMA scheme houses the building program in a complex that includes two iconic towers and a media park. The new CCTV headquarters building forms a monumental bent bridgelike structure, housing administration as well as news, broadcasting, and program production studios. The second structure, the Television Cultural Building, houses a hotel, a visitor's center, a large public theater, and exhibition spaces. The Media Park forms a landscape of public entertainment and outdoor screening facilities.

The OMA scheme asks the question: What makes a landmark today? In a context of competing urban gestures, each striving to be unique, instead of striving for vertical expression, the OMA scheme bends the tower at its midpoint and grounds it to form a loop. The new loop-tower consolidates the building program elements within a structure containing "the entire process of TV making—in a sequence of interconnected activities." The loop defines a dense urban place, as opposed to an isolated tower, which marks a point in the sky.

Developed in conjunction with engineer Cecil Balmond, the OMA loop tower manifests its structural systems on the facade, with an irregular grid corresponding to the forces traveling throughout its structure. Koolhaas's proposal for CCTV's headquarters demonstrates the application of some of OMA's recent research in the rapid urbanization of China, as well as early writings about the skyscraper as an "incubator of new cultures, programs, and ways of life." Koolhaas's loop-tower reinvents the tower to rescue it from its own isolation from the city.

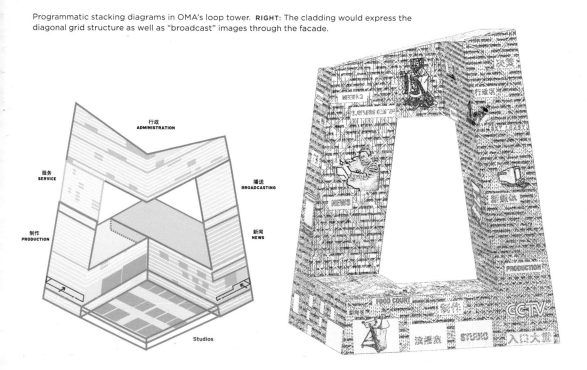

Programmatic stacking diagrams in OMA's loop tower. **RIGHT:** The cladding would express the diagonal grid structure as well as "broadcast" images through the facade.

OMA's winning proposal for the CCTV headquarters in Beijing reinvents the skyscraper as a compact loop, thereby rescuing it from its isolation from the city and from itself.

Folding over its own shaft, the loop tower defines a three-dimensional urban void.
ABOVE: Section through the L-shaped shaft and bridge.

The CCTV loop tower in relation to the adjacent residential structure. **BELOW:** View from within the loop tower's diagonal exterior frame.

DENTSU TOWER
Jean Nouvel, Tokyo 2003

The newly completed Dentsu tower in Tokyo, designed
by Jean Nouvel, creates an ephemeral monument. It
exploits surface effects first proposed for the Tour
Sans Fins project for Paris, where the tower was meant
to dematerialize towards the top. The tower is part of
a new urban development near Tokyo station, on land
formerly occupied by the railway company. The tower
will house the Japanese advertising company Dentsu.

The airfoil-shaped tower appears different from
every angle. Its sculpted mass and rounded corners
emphasize the streamline effect, likening it to the
aerodynamic forms of aircraft and racing cars.

Clad in a taut glass curtain wall, printed with varying densities of gray screens, the tower's significant
mass is rendered obscure, its edges blurry. The distinc-
tions between vision and spandrel glass are obscured
by the screen pattern. Instead of a horizontally banded
appearance, the tower's facade seems to fade in and
out. Its surface effects blur the distinction between
inside and outside, rendering its limits ambiguous.

A large internal atrium extends the height of the
tower. The atrium is lined with stainless-steel bands
that bounce light into the atrium, creating kaleidoscopic effects. Glass-enclosed elevators, located along the
perimeter of the atrium, visible from inside and outside,
animate the tower.

The skyscraper, the aircraft, and the racing car
share the notion that form is a function of performance. In the case of Dentsu Tower, performance is
less a function of speed and displacement, but rather
of effect. The tower is a sleek machine, creating urban
scale effects through the mercurial properties of its
form and cladding.

Tour Dentsu's sculpted mass and rounded corners emphasize a streamline effect, likening it to the aerodynamic forms of aircraft and racing cars.

The airfoil-shaped tower appears different from every angle. **OPPOSITE, TOP:** The Dentsu tower in the Tokyo skyline. **OPPOSITE, BOTTOM:** Instead of a horizontally banded appearance, the tower's facade seems to fade in and out.

kinetic

Kinetic skyscrapers are formally dynamic structures that visually and physically inscribe a process of movement and transformation into a static structure. The implied movement, process, or activity makes the building appear to be caught in motion—a freeze-frame. These projects derive their forms from a design process that employs strategies of formal manipulation, such as shearing, rotating, slipping, or torquing.

While their designs may share a dynamic quality, the reasons for applying kinetic strategies vary widely. The idea of a dynamic architectural form may have its origins in the modern movement, where architects sought to create a new architecture appropriate to the time they were living in. The ocean liner and the automobile became models for modern architecture. Some of the projects in this chapter are motivated by a similar desire to accurately reflect the *zeitgeist*, or spirit of the age.

Radical formal solutions exemplified by "Deconstructivist" architecture sought to critique the stability of architecture and the purity of its forms. According to Mark Wigley, "this is an architecture of disruption, deflection, deviation, and distortion, rather than one of demolition, dismantling, decay, decomposition, or disintegration."[1] To the modernist motto of

fig 1 Coop Himmelb(l)au's GPA Gasometer project.

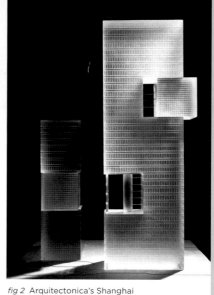

fig 2 Arquitectonica's Shanghai Information Town.

"form follows function," Wigley argues that in these projects, "form follows deformation."[2]

The GPA Gasometer tower, designed by the Austrian firm of Coop Himmelb(l)au is motivated by the desire to create dynamic architecture that is critical of conventions and celebrates the complexity and diversity of contemporary society. [fig 1] The tower's form is simultaneously curved and angular, appearing to tilt and lean on the adjacent building.

Several of the projects in this chapter can be defined by an action or process. The strategy of "folding" drives the designs of the Dong Bu Tower and the Roppongi Tower. As a design strategy, folding comes out of a formal language, but also acknowledges the two-dimensional quality of the cladding. The folded planes on Dong Bu Tower are expressed on their ends with lapped corners to emphasize the planarity of the fold. The sloping glass planes appear frozen in a state of transformation or collapse. Their precarious disposition animates the building and actively engages the viewer.

Some buildings employ a language of "slipped" elements to draw relationships between their parts. The implied movement of parts of Shanghai Information Town Tower suggests that a cube has been slid out of a bar building. [fig 2] The cantilevered cube aligns with a similar-sized void in an adjacent building. The relationship between the elements ties the two buildings together and creates a spatial tension between the parts. An interlocking vocabulary is also employed in the Hotel Nova Diagonal in Barcelona, allowing it to address its context with the lower bar by aligning it with the predominant building height. The implied vertical slip of the hotel bar gives the tower a vertical thrust that accentuates its height.

The implied rotation of Torqued Tower, designed by Santiago Calatrava, and the Parkhaven Tower, designed by Kohn Pedersen Fox, gives both towers an organic quality, whereby they appear to grow out of the ground. The rotation in the Torqued Tower reinforces the structural diagram of twisting vertebrae. The spiraling forms give these buildings added structural strength but also create a dynamic visual effect. [fig 3]

The complexity of some recent skyscrapers reflects the increased use of the computer as a design tool. Many of the projects in this chapter would never have been built without computer-aided design and 3D-modeling software.

Kinetic structures transform process into performance, incorporating implied movements and geometric complexities to produce dramatic effects. The resulting geometries of these slipped, torqued, folded, and crushed buildings produce uneasiness and delight, and therein derive their drama and their force.

1 Mark Wigley, *Deconstructivist Architecture*, The Museum of Modern Art, New York, 1988, p. 17.

2 Ibid., p. 19.

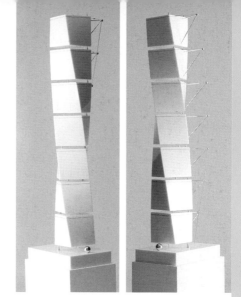

fig 3 Sculpture-study for Santiago Calatrava's Turning Torso.

HOTEL NOVA DIAGONAL
Dominique Perrault, Barcelona, 2004

Dominique Perrault's design for a new hotel along Barcelona's Nova Diagonal consists of a dynamic composition of slab elements suspended in the process of slipping past one another. Perrault conceived of the hotel as a composition made up of two parts: one horizontal, relating to the low scale of the existing city fabric; and the second vertical, relating to the monumental scale of the civic landmarks.

The horizontal podium will house the hotel's public spaces, including the lobby, conference rooms, swimming pool, and bar. The upright vertical slab will house the hotel rooms, each with a view towards either the sea or the mountains. The lobby is entered across a bridge that spans a sunken garden, which corresponds to the footprint of the hotel bar hovering above. The underside of the suspended bar aligns with the top of the podium roof, creating the sense that the individual parts of the tower have slipped and then interlocked like a giant jigsaw puzzle.

The tower was designed to be clad in a system of metal panels, perforated with an array of circular windows. The slender slab refuses the familiar grid of mullions and glass, appearing instead as a porous and diaphanous volume. The windows consist of red, blue, and green glass distributed randomly across the facade, creating the effect of a large stained-glass window. From within the hotel rooms, Barcelona will be viewed through the array of circular windows, transforming the city into a framed mosaic.

Perrault's implied tectonic slippages give the viewer the sense that the tower is frozen in a moment of transformation. The gestures of its implied movement allow the tower to create relationships to its urban context, while the use of porous materials gives the impression of dramatic weightlessness.

LEFT: The front vertical slab houses the hotel rooms, while the lower podium block houses public and convention facilities. **RIGHT:** The circular windows of the hotel frame views of the city, and give the tower a lightweight and porous appearance. **OPPOSITE:** Dominique Perrault's dynamic composition of slipped-and-suspended volumes creates a new landmark for Barcelona.

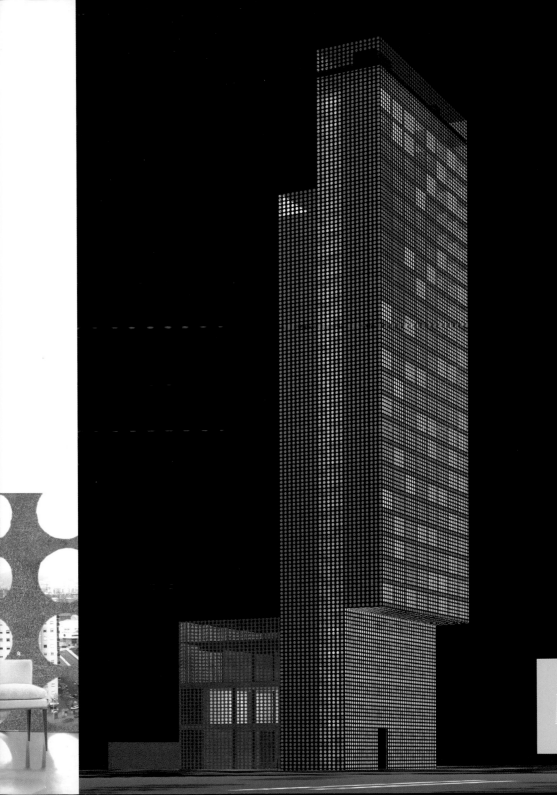

TORQUED TOWER
Santiago Calatrava, Malmö, 2003

Santiago Calatrava, the virtuoso engineer/architect known for his sculptural, biomorphically inspired structures, is currently designing a high-rise residential tower in Malmö, Sweden. Calatrava's structures often find inspiration in nature: the intricate skeletal frame of a canine for example, or the gentle curve of a flower's stem.

The design for the Malmö tower, inspired by a kinetic sculpture, is made up of nine discrete five-story blocks that seem to twist as they rise, evoking the imagery of flexing vertebrae. The tear-shaped blocks are organized around a cylindrical central spine that houses the elevators. Each block houses five residential units, with their kitchens and bathrooms clustered around the vertical nucleus. Each block of five floors twists in relation to its adjacent blocks, resulting in a ninety-degree rotation over the tower's fifty-four floors.

The construction of the tower follows from the concept of employing the concrete service core as

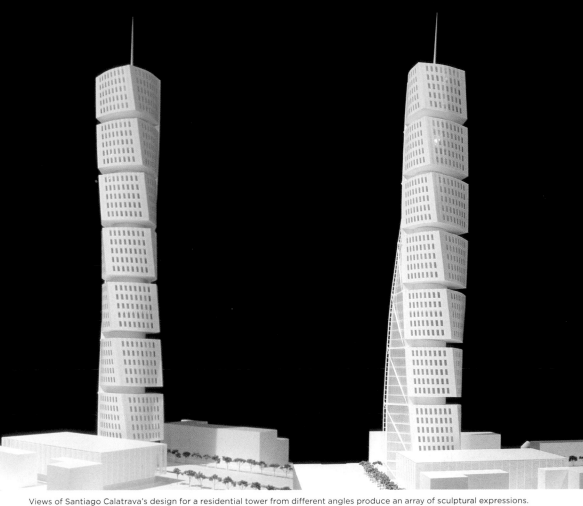

Views of Santiago Calatrava's design for a residential tower from different angles produce an array of sculptural expressions. **BELOW:** The tower performs a dynamic rotation as it rises.

a structural armature. The core and slabs are built first, followed by prefabricated residential enclosures that are attached to the spine, and then by a steel exo-skeleton that traces the outer arc connecting the prow of each floorplate.

Calatrava's work blends structure and gesture, in which the expression of the structural load path is rendered elegantly sculptural. For Calatrava, the two cannot be separated: the efficiency of the structure is embodied in the gesture.

The botanically-inspired Parkhaven tower will be the tallest structure in Europe when completed. Kohn Pedersen Fox International's design for Parkhaven tower is derived from a rotational transformation along the tower's triangular shaft. OPPOSITE: The tower's structural system is "woven" together to form a mesh-like perimeter tube capable of following the tower's dynamic massing.

PARKHAVEN TOWER
Kohn Pedersen Fox Associates International, Rotterdam, 2002 (designed)

The design for Parkhaven Tower, a new high-rise development along the River Maas in Rotterdam, is derived from a design process that involves the gentle transformation of the tower's shaft as it rises. The mixed-use tower will house office functions at the base and residential accommodations above. It will be a focal point of the new master plan for the area and, when complete, will become Europe's tallest tower.

The tower's dramatic spiraling form is derived from a torqued triangular plan. The design is based on an equilateral triangle, in which each side of the triangle has been modified into a compound curve. The tower's form is derived by tapering and rotating the triangular footprint of the tower as it rises. The resulting form is sculpturally bold and vaguely biomorphic.

The tower was conceived with the help of extensive computer-modeling software, which allows the design of complex forms that would have been difficult to document with conventional two-dimensional tools. The tapering and torquing of the tower are modeled, manipulated, and visualized in the computer. Complex three-dimensional forms can be documented and quantified in the construction process by sophisticated software that is shared with the contractors.

At the base, the building's skin peels away to create petal-like canopies. These botanical references inform the massing of the tower and the articulation of its elements. Processes like flowering, blooming, sprouting, and rotating are generative of the tower's language.

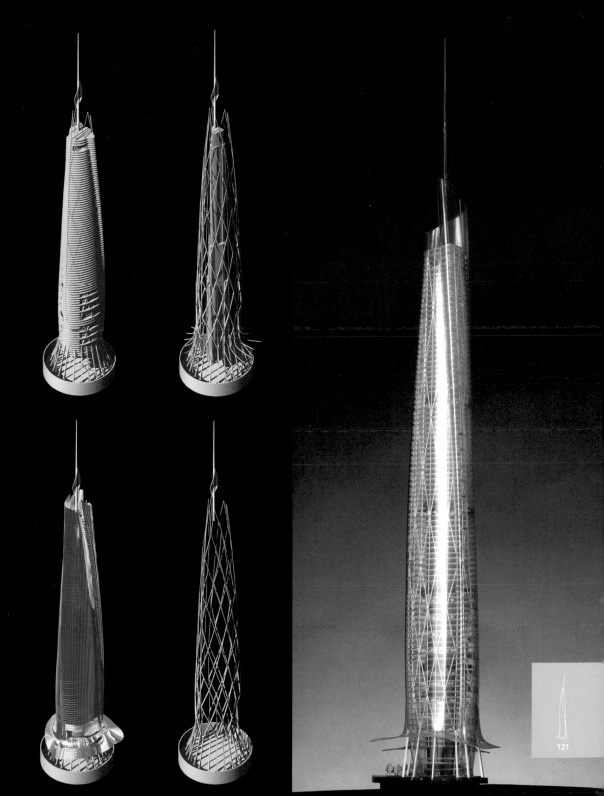

MAAS TOWERS
Archi-Tectonics, Rotterdam, 2003

The three slender towers cantilevered over the Maas River are part of a larger redevelopment of Maashaven, a former industrial section of Rotterdam. The renovation of an existing grain silo and the addition of three new towers will create live-work units that are expected to revitalize this part of the city.

The slender glass towers are faceted bars that cantilever over the river, and then fold, as if inflected by the current of the river. The designer, Winka Dubbeldam, describes the design process as stretching the tower's footprint into a bar, then realigning it to the solar azimuth. The final stage involves the "programmatic inflation" of the bar to arrive at its final tapered form. The "modulation" of the towers is thus relative to the river's current and the sun's position.

Each thirty-story bar is cantilevered from the pier's edge and anchored by a concrete base and service core elements. The towers house split-level, double-height living units. The buildings' facades consist of a taut glass skin that reflects both the river's surface and the city center across the river.

The existing grain silo, dating back to the 1930s, will be renovated to house office space, while the courtyard will contain tennis courts, a running track, and a fitness club.

Dubbeldam's interest in a "trans-formal" architecture is manifested in a dynamic architectural system capable of accommodating what she calls a "spatial fluidity" engendered by technological change in an information society. Dubbeldam's Maas Towers engage the existing city through a carefully orchestrated design process, creating elegant glass structures that are responsive to ephemeral phenomena in the city, ranging from urban transformations resulting from deindustrialization to subtle shifts in solar orientation, water currents, and visual reflections.

Plan of the renovated grain silo and inflected towers jutting out into the river. The tower footprints are faceted to accommodate program and respond to site phenomena.

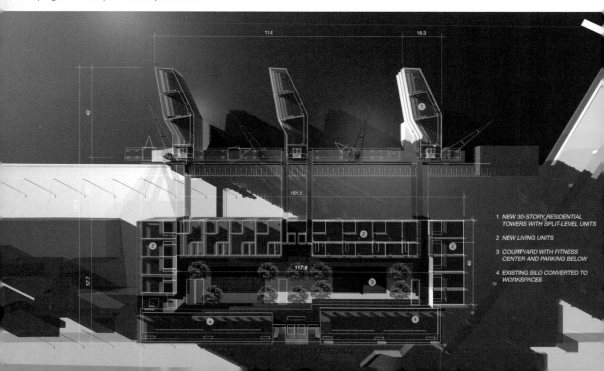

1 NEW 30-STORY RESIDENTIAL TOWERS WITH SPLIT-LEVEL UNITS

2 NEW LIVING UNITS

3 COURTYARD WITH FITNESS CENTER AND PARKING BELOW

4 EXISTING SILO CONVERTED TO WORKSPACES

The dramatic cantilevered slabs hover over the Maas River, responding to natural and urban phenomena through the disposition of their form and optical properties of their enclosure.

DONG BU HEADQUARTERS
Kohn Pedersen Fox Associates, Seoul, 2002

Designed as the new headquarters for a Korean insurance company, Dong Bu Tower expresses the confidence and exuberance of the pre-1997 Asian economic boom. Employing a language of angular planes, the designers created a dynamic form that distinguishes it from the other office towers lining Teheran Road in Seoul, Korea.

The tower's form is a play on the sharply defined "street wall" of Teheran Road. While most buildings stand on the property line to maximize their bulk, Dong Bu Tower sits towards the back of the site to create a small urban plaza that acts like a pedestal from which to view the building as a sculptural object.

The broad face of the tower is made up of a series of sloped, folded planes, which make the tower appear to be undergoing a process of transformation. Unlike most skyscrapers that result from a repetition of standard floorplate sizes, the sloping walls of the primary facade make each of Dong Bu's thirty-five stories unique.

The building cladding reinforces the planar reading of the building mass, emphasizing the "grain" of the building. All the east and west walls are clad in blue glass with closely spaced horizontal stainless-steel mullions. At the corners, these walls extend beyond the edge of the building, reinforcing their planar reading by presenting an exposed edge of the surface. The north and south walls are clad in a taut clear glass with corrugated shadow boxes in the spandrel areas.

The ground-floor lobby is linked to the subway system and to an underground retail network. Escalators take the visitor up to the limestone- and wood-clad lobby. A decorative glass storefront wall, derived from traditional Korean quilting patterns, allows diffused light into the lobby.

Sacrificing repetition and efficiency for dramatic form, the design for the Dong Bu headquarters embodies the aspirations of many Asian skyscrapers prior to 1997. The tower's bold sculptural form sets it apart from the city fabric, making it a signature landmark building.

TOP: A taut glass curtain wall stretches between the folded planes, emphasizing the "grain" of the building. **BOTTOM:** The densely spaced horizontal mullions articulate the broad faces of the tower.

Dong Bu Headquarters viewed from Teheran Road creates a dramatic composition of folding glass planes.

125

POSTEEL HEADQUARTERS TOWER
Kohn Pedersen Fox Associates, Seoul, 2003

Designed as a corporate headquarters for Posteel, a large Korean steel manufacturer, the tower is a powerful sculpted emblem for the company. Located on a prominent intersection on Teheran Road, the tower gestures towards the corner, where the building mass is sliced away to create a dramatic prismatic form that hovers over the entrance.

The design of the tower is derived from a language of bent steel plates, celebrating the industry and manufacturing processes of the company housed within. The architects describe the design process as an exercise in "folding and assembly" of metal panels. The cladding design articulates the corner prow figure as a sleek, reflective volume, while the body of the building is treated with a dense horizontal texture of stainless-steel-clad mullions.

The structural steel frame reinforces the primary diagonal thrust of the prow by allowing the corner to cantilever over the entrance without any vertical supports. Diagonal structural members are visible behind the curtain wall, accentuating the corner. Far from being a neutral steel cage, the structural system is the primary sculptural gesture.

The design of this dramatic faceted tower is derived from a process of cutting and folding surfaces, revealing the seams were surfaces meet and creating contrasting patterns on the surface of the building. Employing this design vocabulary, the architects produced a design that is both visually dramatic and rigorously derived.

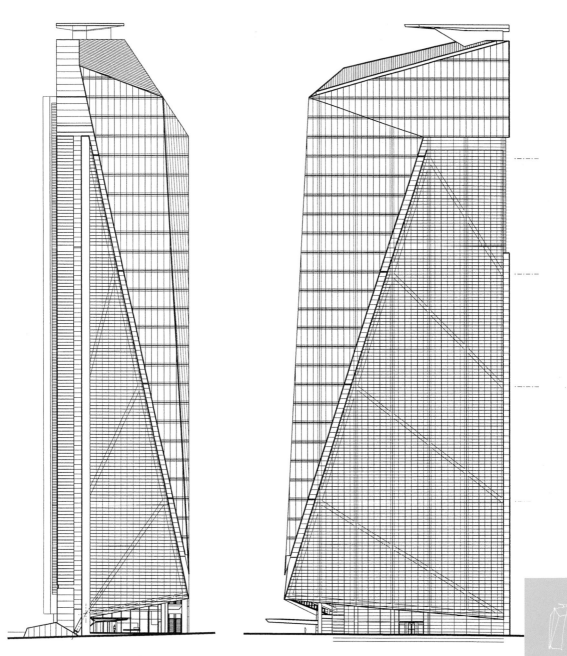

East and North elevations. **OPPOSITE:** The angular form of Posteel Tower has a metallurgical source—the bent steel plates manufactured by Posteel Corporation.

ROPPONGI TOWER
Kohn Pedersen Fox Associates, Tokyo, 2003

The Roppongi Tower forms the massive centerpiece of a twenty-seven-acre urban redevelopment project in the heart of Tokyo's Roppongi retail and entertainment district. The fifty-eight-story tower will house three million square feet of office space in its shaft and an art museum at its top. Also part of the development is a 550-room hotel, a performing arts theater, and a shopping mall.

The tower derives its unusual shape from a design process that is dictated by its immense size. The tower is so large that the city authorities feared that it would disrupt the television broadcast signal from Tokyo Tower. The design brief stipulated that the tower's mass should be broken down to avoid flat surfaces that would create signal reflections and broadcast shadows.

The architects looked to origami for a language of folded planes that could inform the shape of the tower. In plan, the tower is an oblong shape made up of various curved line segments that crease and peel, breaking up the tower's mass. The base of the tower's shaft is gathered through a series of facets to accommodate the larger public facilities. The tower's articulated crown will house the Mori Art Center in its top five floors.

The curtain wall consists of lightly reflective glass and painted, pre-cast concrete panels. The material selection was designed to avoid metallic surfaces that would reflect the television waves.

The sculpted mass of the tower minimizes its presence through the selection of its materials and the manipulation of its surface. The tower employs strategies analogous to those of the Stealth Bomber, which is invisible to radar due to its angular geometry.

The largest building in Japan, Roppongi Tower's massive form dominates the skyline.

Roppongi Tower under construction. **BELOW**: Roppongi Tower nearing completion. **OPPOSITE**: The curves of Roppongi Tower were designed to deflect radio waves and television signals.

GPA GASOMETER TOWER
Coop Himmelb(l)au, Vienna, 2001

Wolf Prix and Helmut Siczinsky founded the avant-garde practice of Coop Himmelblau in 1968. The name Himmelblau, or heavens-blue, suggests heroic or utopian aspirations, and their designs have ignited architecture debates through their manifestos and radical designs. In a 1980 manifesto, Prix challenges conventional building design: "Architecture should be cavernous, fiery, smooth, hard, angular, brutal, round, delicate, colorful, obscene, voluptuous, dreamy, alluring, repelling, wet, dry, and throbbing. Alive or dead. Cold—then cold as a block of ice. Hot—then hot as a blazing wing. Architecture must blaze."[1]

Recently, the firm has been winning competitions and building its visionary designs, prompting the architects to change their name from Himmelblau to Himmelb(l)au, or heavens-build. One of their first large realized projects is the GPA Gasometer tower, which, true to their radical imagery, has a distinctly impacted form.

As part of the redevelopment of Vienna's industrial quarters, the government held a series of competitions for the reuse and redevelopment of several large and obsolete infrastructure works. Coop Himmelb(l)au won the commission to transform a series of classically designed former gas containers into a mixed-use complex of shopping, office, and residential structures.

The existing industrial structure is converted into radial residential units, while a new structure is located on the northern side. The new structure, a bent curvilinear slab, echoes the cylinder, but interprets it in new materials and new geometries. Its combination of facets and curves suggests a deformation of a familiar form, rather than the presence of something altogether new. The design is interpretive of its context, the result of a formal process of deformation and transformation.

Coop Himmelb(l)au's design vocabulary does not attempt to create a pure sculptural form. Instead, it appears to be the outcome of a disjunctive process, whereby building forms are subjected to a formal manipulation that renders them intricate and complex. In the words of the architects, "Architecture for our time must reflect the complexity and variety of modern society."[2] At the time of their founding, the world may not have been ready for their radical vision of architecture. Today, many of their architectural provocations have been realized, and their complex vocabulary has entered the lexicon of architectural styles.

1 Wolf D. Prix, *On the Edge,* in *Architecture in Transition,* Peter Noever, Munich, 1991, p. 31.

2 Prix, p. 20.

GPA Gasometer's sloped and bent form appears to lean on the structure of the existing gas building. **OPPOSITE**: the convex facade of GPA Gasometer recalls the drumlike form of existing gas plant, creating a sculptural "echo" of the original.

GPA Gasometer is part of a redevelopment of Vienna's industrial quarters, renovating existing infrastructure for new uses.

scenographic

At the 1929 Beaux Arts Ball, William van Allen, the designer of the Chrysler Building, masqueraded as his landmark skyscraper, which was then being built. Van Allen's elaborate costume, complete with his signature spire headdress, underscores the theatrical dimension of the skyscraper and the role it has played in the theater of the urban skyline. [Figs 1, 2] The Chrysler Building and the Empire State Building were some of the first protagonists in the unfolding drama of the city. These early skyscrapers dressed structural steel frames in elaborate cladding, transforming the mundane into the spectacular. The New York skyline in 1929 was an urban stage set, complete with skyscraper cathedrals and temples, elaborate scenes and costumes, illusionist distortions, and vanishing acts.

The contemporary city finds itself in a state of transformation, as whole neighborhoods are redeveloped. For example, the "New Times Square" has transformed from a sleazy neighborhood into a family entertainment zone. The architecture of Times Square serves as the illuminated backdrop to the new media-saturated public sphere. Increasingly, urban centers are transformed into themed entertainment environments.

fig 1 William van Allen, architect of the Chrysler building, in costume at the Beaux Arts Ball, 1929.

fig 2 The Chrysler Building. Architecture as costume.

Las Vegas epitomizes the scenographic trend in architecture, feeding the public's insatiable appetite for the spectacular. The New York, New York Hotel in Las Vegas incorporates the Empire State Building and the Statue of Liberty into a compact theatrical composition. The hotel disguises one building in the costume of many buildings, forming the backdrop for a parade of elaborate urban fantasies. [fig 3]

Scenographic skyscrapers participate in the urban theater as actors and stage sets. These skyscrapers participate in the theater of the city wearing elaborate costumes to blend in or stand out, distinguishing themselves through their spires and crowns, their masks and cloaks. The scenographic skyscraper exploits the dramatic potential of the facade as mask, where curtain-wall building enclosures act as theatrical scenery.

The Austrian Cultural Forum, designed by Raimund Abraham, evokes strong associations with a totemic mask through its anthropomorphic qualities. [fig 4] The cascading composition of glass and metal planes appears suspended in mid-collapse—a structural performance in steel and concrete.

The DG Bank Headquarters also plays a choreographed role in the city by participating in a dialogue with the urban context. Its carefully considered massing addresses various neighborhoods, orientations and scales. Dressed in its radial crown and crisp, white cladding, the tower occupies the role of prima donna in Frankfurt's elaborate skyscraper

fig 3 The New York, New York Hotel posits costume as an urbanism.

pageant. *[fig 5]*

A more explosive urban theater is unfolding in many Asian cities, where the skyscraper is drafted into the service of creating new urban landmarks. Cities like Shanghai, Shenzhen, and Guangzhou have undergone tremendous growth over the past fifteen years, and further growth is expected in the near future. The skyscraper is the principal component of the urban transformation of Asian cities. It is often invested with grand aspirations, constructing the requisite image of progress and modernity. In doing so, the new structures tend toward the exuberant and the spectacular, employing decorative motifs, ornamental crowns, gaudy materials and polychromatic lighting.

The skyscraper is built spectacle. It is a lead actor in the contemporary city, distinguishing itself through theatrical gestures and applied features. These buildings are often mannerist in their designs, supplementing their structures with the novel and the unexpected. Designers of skyscrapers are acutely aware of the expressive potential of these urban protagonists.

fig 4 The Austrian Cultural Forum evokes strong
associations with a totemic mask through its anthropomorphic qualities.

fig 5 DG Bank.

LEFT: The "mask" of the building along 51st Street follows the prescribed setback zoning envelope. RIGHT: The entrance canopy under the cascading glass planes. OPPOSITE: The symmetrical composition of Raimund Abraham's Austrian Cultural Forum gives the tower a distinctly anthropomorphic appearance.

AUSTRIAN CULTURAL FORUM
Raimund Abraham, New York, 2002

The Austrian Cultural Forum, designed by Raimund Abraham, is a striking new addition to New York's urban theater. Its completion, ten years after the design was unveiled, has evoked images of totems, masks, guillotines, and metronomes.

The facade, composed of five sloping, glass-clad panels that overlap one another, creates the effect of cascading glass shingles. The panels are punctuated by a series of symmetrical features that either project out or are carved in, giving the facade a distinctly anthropomorphic appearance. Abraham uses anthropomorphic terms to describe the tower's three parts: the vertebra at the back, the core at its center, and the mask facing the street.

The narrow site, twenty-five feet wide and eighty-one feet deep, dictated the slender proportions. The slopes follow the New York zoning setback requirements, but Abraham did not merely comply with the zoning requirements—his design dramatizes the

building envelope in a spectacle of sharp geometry and precarious structure. "I tried to develop a tectonic vocabulary that would not make the tower rise, but rather the opposite; the point was to make it fall—that falling notion projected the sense of suspension."[1]

The forum houses the cultural arm of the Austrian Ministry of Foreign Affairs. The building contains a variety of program elements, compactly stacked in the vertical section: exhibition space, a lounge/café, a library, a theater, offices, and a residence for the director and his family.

Although technically not a skyscraper by conventional definitions, the Austrian Cultural Forum's dramatic shape and sliverlike proportions create a powerful visual impact, challenging the conventional limits of the building type.

1 Raimund Abraham, in *Technology, Place & Architecture*, Kenneth Frampton, ed., Rizzoli, New York, 1998, p. 26.

1250 BOULEVARD RENÉ LEVESQUE
Kohn Pedersen Fox Associates, Montreal, 1992

Regarded as a classic example of a contextual skyscraper, this forty-seven-story office building derives its form from a dialogue with its surroundings. Located in Montreal's central business district, adjacent to the landmark Windsor Station and one block from Dorchester Square, the tower's massing is sensitive to the historical urban fabric while projecting the iconic image of a multinational corporation on the skyline.

The composition breaks the building into distinct parts that correspond to the specific site orientation and scale of the urban fabric. From a distance, the building appears to be a compositional interplay of curved and orthogonal volumes. The orthogonal stone-clad volumes face west and serve as the support armature for the east-facing curved glass-and-aluminum volume. At the base, the building mass is stepped to relate to the smaller scale of the existing city fabric. The low-scale elements of the building podium shelter a landscaped plaza, which occupies the northeast corner of the site. Adjacent to the plaza is a six-story winter garden that also serves as the building's entrance from the boulevard. The building is capped by a cantilevered horizontal visor, which gestures south towards the river.

The building mass is stitched together by the articulated design of the curtain wall, which weaves the horizontal spandrel fabric through the vertical stone piers. The stone piers give the orthogonal mass a visual weight reminiscent of Rockefeller Center. The horizontal bands of the curved glass volume give the building an appearance of lightness, creating a dramatic tension between the dynamic and static elements.

The project marks a transitional period for Kohn Pedersen Fox, who established their reputation for designs derived from external contextual forces and internal programmatic needs. The project departs from the historicist language of postmodernism with a shift towards what William Pedersen has called "theatrical"[1] modernism.

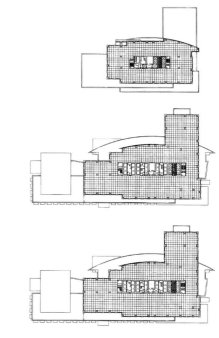

1 William Pedersen quoted by Bradford McKee in "Towering Ambitions: KPF Charts a New Course," *Architecture*, November 1997, p. 96.

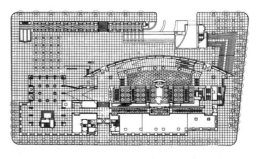

ABOVE: The winter garden and paved plaza create a forecourt to the tower. **CENTER:** Ground floor, mezzanine, and low-rise office plans. **BELOW:** Site plan.

Kohn Pedersen Fox's 1250 Boulevard René-Lévesque Ouest presents a contextual approach to skyscraper design, with each of the tower's parts articulated to respond to internal and external conditions.

DG BANK
Kohn Pedersen Fox Associates, Frankfurt, 1993

The 658-foot (201 meter) DG Bank Headquarters is one of the first American-style skyscrapers to be built in a European city, where building regulations had traditionally limited building heights. The design of the DG Bank allows this American import to integrate itself into the city fabric by breaking the tower into a composition of discrete parts.

Composed of distinct masses, the design introduces a new "tower of three parts." Each of its parts—podium, shaft, and crown—is molded by external site forces and internal programmatic needs. In this case, the design brief called for a mix of uses, including office space, residential apartments, and a central winter garden. The design of the tower includes a slender shaft with a low-rise podium that wraps around the winter garden. The low-rise structure embraces the winter garden and defines the perimeter of the block. The tower takes on a figural quality in the shaft, and creates a signature profile against the sky, where a radial, cantilevered crown gestures towards the old center of Frankfurt.

This marriage of curvilinear and rectilinear volumes places the tower in dialogue with its external context, while its internal spatial requirement for natural light informs the tower's slender proportions. The materials used to clad the tower reinforce each separate element. The shaft of the tower is made up of a curved volume, clad in white metal and glass, while the orthogonal volume is clad in stone, with punched openings. The central volume, an exterior expression of the service core, is clad in stone and acts as an organizing spine. The low-rise perimeter blocks are clad primarily in stone with punched-out windows to help ground the tower.

Stylistically, the DG Bank tower is a pivotal building, marking the climax of a collagist design strategy of assembly of discrete building parts, and signaling a shift away from classically inspired postmodernism, towards a language that could be called "theatrical modernism." The design of the tower harkens to a romantic age of skyscraper design, when each building was a theatrical actor in an elaborate urban masquerade. The DG Bank tower's architectural articulations and formal gestures place the building in dialogue with its audience—the city.

DG Bank's collagist approach to design produces
a skyscraper as an assembly of discrete parts,
each articulated to address its audience, the city.
OPPOSITE, LEFT: The interior courtyard.
OPPOSITE, RIGHT: At the base, a low rise podium
embraces a public winter garden.

The decorative crown atop Plaza 66.

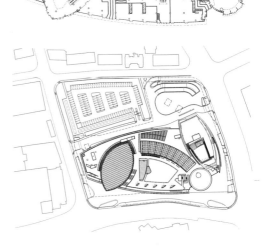

Typical podium plan and site plan.

PLAZA 66
Kohn Pedersen Fox Associates, Shanghai, 2001

Located along Nanjing Xi Lu, Shanghai's historical commercial street, the new mixed-use development draws on the vibrant street life to inform the vocabulary of building elements. Its voluptuous composition of curvilinear forms makes it approach the baroque.

The development is comprised of two office towers and a five-story retail podium that houses a luxury shopping mall. The design is based on a language of concave and convex geometry that shapes each of the major building elements. The mall is organized around a curved retail gallery, which connects an almond-shaped atrium to an inverted-cone-shaped volume. The towers are arranged radially around an implied center, and share a curved mid-height bridge. Each volume is articulated as distinct and recognizable, composed sculpturally as a three-dimensional collage. The architects describe the dynamic composition as an "Embrace of swirling forms . . .influenced by the forces of a vortex."

Each element in the composition is clad in a distinct curtain-wall fabric. The retail podium is clad in stone, while the shafts of the two towers are clad in a vertically articulated glass curtain wall. The upward spiral of the composition is terminated by a translucent glass lantern. The need to surmount a tower with a dramatic crown, spire, or headpiece is typical of theatrical Asian skyscrapers, and is a reference to early Art Deco skyscrapers like the Empire State Building and the Chrysler Building.

The project is typical of a crop of buildings that sprang up in Shanghai in the late 1990s. Fueled by optimism, foreign investment, and departure from traditionally strict speculative office space criteria, these projects embraced a formal exuberance unseen anywhere else in the world. The cumulative effect of these developments have transformed the city, and reestablished an image of Shanghai as the cultural and business center of a new China.

Plaza 66's voluptuous composition of curvilinear forms are characteristic of the formal exuberance that transformed Shanghai into the cultural and business center of China.

Shun Hing Square, designed in two months and constructed in forty months. The tower is a symbol of China's instant urbanism—a relentless attempt to achieve modernity through rapid urbanization.

SHUN HING SQUARE
K. Y. Cheung Design Associates, Shenzhen, 1996

On the border between Hong Kong and the southern Chinese province of Guandong is Shenzhen, a city that twenty years ago had a population of 30,000, but has swelled to between four and six million inhabitants today. It is referred to as an "instant city" in the constellation of cities in the Pearl River Delta. Standing at the crossroads of a major intersection in Shenzhen is Shun Hing Square.

At sixty-nine stories tall, 1263 feet (385 meters), Shun Hing Plaza is the eleventh-tallest building in the world. Approaching the Guandong border by train from Hong Kong, the viewer is surrounded by fields of green, which are in stark contrast to the urban density of Hong Kong. Then suddenly, as the train rounds a bend, Shun Hing Square rises like a needle from the fields in the foreground. As one gets closer, the full impact of Shenzhen is felt. The city rises like a dense urban forest pushing up against the Shenzhen River, which marks the border with the New Territories.

The building's architect, K. Y. Cheung, states that the tower was designed and constructed in record time: two months for design and forty months for construction. The accelerated schedule is typical of the instant urbanism of southern China. The mixed use development is made up of a shopping mall, an apartment block, and a office tower with an observation deck at the top. Cheung sought to articulate each element differently, choosing distinct materials for each part. The tower is clad in a green reflective glass; the residential bar is clad in white tiles with a rotated element clad in red; and the retail mall is clad in granite, overlayed with a rotated-grid pattern.

The tower footprint consists of a glass lozenge shape intersected with a stone-clad rectangular volume. The curved corners make it sleek and futuristic, while the rectilinear areas are efficient and easily leased. The tower is remarkable for its slender proportions, with a width to height ratio of 1:9, pushing the limits of structural engineering. The cylinders are expressed as spires at the top with a tilted volume appearing like a keystone cap.

The image of a skyscraper in a field resonates in the Pearl River Delta, where cities have emerged seemingly overnight as foreign investment capital pours across the border, extending the manufacturing base from Hong Kong to the entire Pearl River Delta region. The economic and cultural forces acting on the built environment in Shenzhen have created an instant urbanism. The forest of towers, many of them without tenants, are a Potemkin Metropolis of China's aspirations of Western modernity.

The border between Shenzhen and Hong Kong's New Territories is marked by an abrupt urban cliff, pushed up against the border.

Shun Hing Square combines an office tower, a retail mall, and a residential portion housed in the adjacent slab. **OPPOSITE:** The distinct articulation of each of the complex's parts is achieved though form and color.

151

INTERNATIONAL FINANCE CENTER 2
Cesar Pelli & Associates, Hong Kong, 2004

This latest addition to the Hong Kong skyline towers above its neighbors, creating a new landmark in a city already saturated with skyscrapers. Together with the Kowloon Station Tower across the water, the two projects will mark the north and south banks of the harbor forming the "harbor gateway."

Part of an ambitious harborfront development, the IFC complex is built over Hong Kong Station, the terminus of the airport express train connecting Hong Kong to its new airport. The complex will contain an 88-story office tower, a 32-story office tower, a Four Seasons Hotel, a retail podium, and links to a new ferry terminal. The complex links with the new Central-Wanchai reclamation, intended to create a new pedestrian promenade on Hong Kong Island's harborfront.

Built on reclaimed land, the new tower extends the central business district, known as Central, to the north. The heart of the city's banking and financial district, Central is also the retail epicenter of Hong Kong. IFC will connect to the existing retail network made up of an intricate web of shopping malls and pedestrian bridges, tying multiple buildings together within a single retail atmosphere.

The International Finance Center 2 dominates Hong Kong's skyline.

The International Finance Center tower draws its inspiration from the Art Deco American skyscrapers. It evokes the setback style of towers in New York and Chicago, and recalls Eliel Saarinen's second-place entry to the *Chicago Herald Tribune* competition. Both designs feature a tapering tower with chiseled corners and an articulated top. A decorative feature, composed of multiple vertical blades, crowns the building and extends the tapered gesture of the tower.

Unlike the early Art Deco buildings, which were clad in stone, this tower is clad in reflective silver glass. The curtain wall is articulated as a vertical shaft, with the curtain-wall members expressed as vertical piers. Intermittent horizontal members weave between the piers and add a fabriclike texture to the skin.

Pelli's design for the International Finance Center creates a dramatic new addition to the Hong Kong skyline by referencing the early skyscraper designs of the Art Deco period. The nostalgic references to early American skyscrapers illustrate Pelli's assertion that a tower is a "true skyscraper" only if it has a "centric form that tapers with well-proportioned setbacks, expressing a vertical movement towards the sky." Everything else is just a high rise.

The building evokes the romantic era of skyscrapers through its tapered shaft, articulated
facade, and decorative crown. **OPPOSITE:**
Detail of the facade and crown.

The Burj al Arab hotel creates a vertical fantasy world in the image of the skyscraper.

BURJ AL ARAB
W.S Atkins, Dubai, 1999

The Burj Al Arab luxury hotel in Dubai creates a vertical fantasy world in the image of the skyscraper. The tower's billowing form and lavish interiors create the setting for an elaborate resort experience.

Built on a man-made island, the hotel is accessed by helicopter or via a private causeway served by the hotel's fleet of Rolls Royces. The skyscraper is the apt vessel for a resort experience predicated on exclusivity.

The tower, inspired by the billowing curves of a sailboat, gesture out to the sea with a prow-shaped tower and a sail-like atrium. The two sides of the triangular plan enclose a full-height atrium, which is enclosed in a taut fiberglass membrane. The articulation of the structure, complete with trusses and masts,

reinforces the nautical metaphors and gives the tower a distinct futuristic appearance.

All the rooms are duplexes with twenty-three-foot (seven meter) floor-to-ceiling heights, for a maximum of spatial and material luxury. A rich palate of materials, inspired by local materials and Arabian literature, is used on the interiors. Fabrics, metalwork, and ornament contribute to the voluptuous interiors.

Appearing like a mirage on the horizon, the new Burj Al Arab hotel is the epitome of extravagance and luxury. It is an extreme building combining opulence in form and color with a theatrical structural expressiveness. It is the paradigm of architecture as a stage set for an elaborate fantasy world.

A choreographed light and sound show transforms the tower into a perpetual spectacle.

mediatic

Historically, the tower has served to communicate to the masses. Cathedrals demonstrated the awe-inspiring power of God through their great height and structural disposition. They also marked the passage of time, through the ringing of their bells. The medieval tower, visible and audible from great distances, served as a communal focus and early form of mass media.

Contemporary towers, though built for different purposes, still communicate varied messages. Their dramatic scale and iconographic status allow them to communicate to a mass audience. At an urban scale they form visual markers and collective symbols. Their presence proliferates through images and icons, making them emblems of corporations, cities, and nations. The Transamerica Pyramid, designed by William Pereira, not only houses the company's headquarters, but it has also become the corporate logo, as well as an instantly recognizable landmark for the city of San Francisco. [fig 1] The Transamerica Corporation achieves an iconic presence through the design of its corporate headquarters, creating recognition value that is hard to quantify. The Petronas Towers in Kuala Lumpur articulates a similar message. By claiming the title of world's tallest building, they

fig 2 The Petronas Towers in Kuala Lumpur.

fig 3 The Empire State Building in New York.

established a presence in the global consciousness as twin icons of the nation's economic aspirations. *[fig 2]* The secular skyscraper is still a powerful form of mass media.

Today, technological innovations that first enabled the skyscraper in curtain wall technology and integrated lighting are now allowing the skyscraper to transform into a multimedia communication apparatus. Early skyscrapers employed seasonal lighting schemes and searchlights to enhance their dramatic effect. The Empire State Building's multicolored lighting scheme broadcasts seasonal and commemorative messages: red, white, and blue on the fourth of July and green on Saint Patrick's Day. *[fig 3]*

Times Square in New York, Picadilly Circus in London, Shinjuku Station in Tokyo, and large areas of Hong Kong Island have transformed whole city districts into all neon epicenters basking in the glow of millions of electric suns. Zoning regulations, designed to preserve the character of Times Square's early Broadway Theater days require new buildings built in the district to incorporate various types of signage and lighting. The seemingly chaotic illuminated landscape that results is, in fact, a highly regulated condition, calculated in watts and lumens. The result is a spectacular urban effect, where the city dissolves in the glare of lights and animated graphics.

Developments in computer-controlled lighting and fiber optic wiring allow architectural surfaces to become full-height

fig 4 The Centre in Hong Kong transforms into a spectacular pyrotechnic display of multicolored lights.

animated screens. Contemporary skyscrapers create spectacular displays with animated lighting programs and large-scale jumbotrons. [figs 4] The podium of 745 Seventh Avenue, designed by Kohn Pedersen Fox Associates, integrates LED technology into the spandrel panels, allowing high-resolution animations to transform the building base into a multistory animated billboard. [fig 5] The animated graphics, designed by Imaginary Forces, can be updated to correspond to new corporate identities, new seasonal colors, or new marketing campaigns. The KPN Telecom tower in Rotterdam, designed by Renzo Piano Building Workshop, takes the concept of a façade as animated screen to a new level, with integrated light fixtures at every façade panel. In this instance, the whole entire façade of the tower becomes a 22-story animated billboard, broadcasting pixilated images across the city.

Contemporary Mediatic skyscrapers manifest a presence in excess of their physical dimensions—a kind of hyper-presence—announcing in spectacular terms the arrival to the global stage of the company or city that erected it. The Centre, in Hong Kong, a banal building by day, transforms into a spectacular pyrotechnic display of multicolored lights at night. The Burj al Arab Hotel in Dubai performs a choreographed show every half-hour, combining fire, water, and lighting features to simulate a volcanic eruption.

The contemporary Mediatic skyscraper is choreographed, not designed. It distinguishes itself from its surroundings by its stature, form, and effect. The emerging trend among Mediatic skyscrapers signals a shift from the purely

fig 5 745 Seventh Avenue in Times Square, designed by Kohn Pedersen Fox, employs large L.E.D. displays integrated into the spandrel panels of the curtain wall.

quantitative (i.e. how tall) to the design of urban effect (i.e. how spectacular). The new skyscrapers act as urban landmarks, but also as an urban phenomenon—they are architecture as built spectacle.

TOUR SANS FINS
Jean Nouvel, Paris, 1989 (designed)

Aptly named the Tour Sans Fins—the Endless Tower—this building creates, along its full height, a singular optical effect: the disappearing act of the tower itself. Starting at its base, which is "carved" out of stone, the tower becomes increasingly transparent as it rises, culminating in a clear glass crown that is meant to fade into the sky.

The materials used to clad the structure form a spectrum from weighty opacity to lightness and transparency. At its base, the tower descends several levels underground like a crater. As it rises, the shaft is clad in a range of materials of graded transparencies: unpolished black granite, anthracite granite, polished mica, polished aluminum, polished stainless-steel, reflective glass, tinted glass, silk-screened glass, and, lastly, clear glass.

The building's slender shaft is circular with a cross-braced perimeter-frame structure. Elevators are located on the perimeter allowing for both a panoramic ascent and the accommodation of open-plan office spaces within the tower. A large pendulum acts as a mass damper to limit building sway in high winds.

According to Nouvel, the role of the architect is analogous to that of the conjurer, in that they both seek to create spectacular dramatic effects: "You don't quite know where the cylinder begins and ends because it rises from an excavation and dissipates into the sky."[1] Contrary to the conventions of skyscrapers, which seek to define a singular presence through architectural form and material, this tower performs the spectacle of its own disappearance.

1 Jean Nouvel, in *Technology Place & Architecture*, Kenneth Frampton, ed., Rizzoli Publishing, New York, 1998, p. 86.

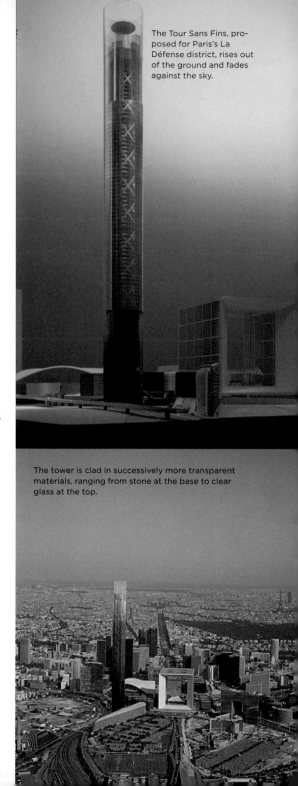

The Tour Sans Fins, proposed for Paris's La Défense district, rises out of the ground and fades against the sky.

The tower is clad in successively more transparent materials, ranging from stone at the base to clear glass at the top.

Rather than presenting an imposing architectural presence, Jean Nouvel's Tour Sans Fins performs the spectacle of its own disappearance through the articulation of its cladding.

5 TIMES SQUARE
Kohn Pedersen Fox Associates,
New York, 2002

Marking the corner of Seventh Avenue and the "New 42nd Street," the 5 Times Square building forms a sleek new addition to the animated architecture of Times Square. The tower's angular massing and diagonal lines play off the visual cacophony of Times Square, generating a design that blends into the context by transforming the architecture into signage.

The mass of the tower is broken down through a series of cuts and folds in the facade, emphasizing a prismatic volume on the corner. The cladding accentuates the prow-shaped corner figure, employing taut silver glass on the corner, and a horizontally banded glass on the sides. A sawtooth horizontal texture creates a radiating patterned overlay on the facade adjacent to the prow. The geometry of the tower avoids right angles, adding to the tower's angular appearance and camouflaging its mass.

Signage bands run up the side of the tower, reinforcing the diagonal peels, and animating the façades. Ernst and Young's illuminated corporate logo crowns the top, while at the base the lower floors are covered in a jumbled assortment of illuminated billboards.

The proliferation of billboards and illuminated signs in Times Square is the result of a zoning regulation, which is rooted in historic preservation and intended to recall the early days of Broadway glitter and neon. The law dictates that new buildings in the Times Square area incorporate a variety of illuminated signs into new designs. The billboards often obscure views from the interiors, but the vertical surfaces get a higher rent per square foot than the horizontal surfaces of the floorplate behind them. Buildings on Times Square act as an armature for the multistory animated billboards.

The explosive and animated graphics that splash across building facades in Times Square create an unprecedented neon landscape. Jumbo televisions and pixilated facades saturate the neighborhood. The new illuminated landscape causes the architecture to dissolve in the glare of lights and mediatized architectural surfaces. Buildings like 5 Times Square embrace the dynamic new media, transforming architecture into ecstatic iconographic images.

5 Times Square's geometry and facade treatment break down the tower's mass into a series of faceted planes.

LVMH TOWER
Christian de Portzamparc, New York, 1999

This slender skyscraper is designed as the American headquarters for the fashion conglomerate Moët Henessey-Louis Vuitton. The twenty-story tower, occupying a slender site on 57th Street, distinguishes itself by departing from the city fabric in its geometry and materiality.

The tower transforms the set-back pyramidal building form derived from the New York City zoning envelope and camouflages it in a series of diaphanous layers of glass. The curtain wall seems to perform a sophisticated striptease with layer upon layer of glass concealing and revealing the building within. Portzamparc uses a combination of glass types and finishes to create the ephemeral effect. Clear, green, and low-iron glass are all used to differentiate the layers. Sand-blasted patterns on the glass create a diagonal pattern on the facade.

At night, the edge of the fold is illuminated with cold cathode lights that shift in color from violet to green to red. As the headquarters for a fashion empire, the LVMH Tower presents itself as an ephemeral, ever-changing image.

In a city driven by orthogonal efficiency and price per square foot, this idiosyncratic jewel of a skyscraper embodies the luxury of geometric complexity in the service of high-style design.

A combination of glass and finishes are employed to make the surfaces of the LVMH tower appear ephemeral and diffuse.
OPPOSITE, LEFT: The facade design creates a delicate composition of folded glass surfaces. **OPPOSITE, RIGHT:**
The building massing interprets New York City's setback zoning regulations as a series of folded layers.

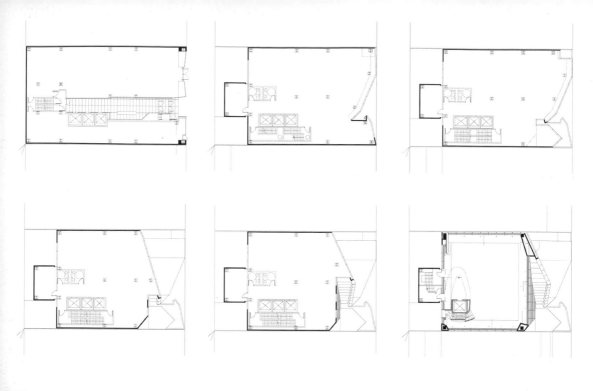

LVMH building framed by its context on 57th Street and Fifth Avenue.
OPPOSITE: Views from within the tower's double-height reception floor.

AIA TOWER
OMA Asia, Hong Kong, 1998

Despite advances made in the realm of structures, materials, and systems, the stylistic evolution of the skyscraper has occurred primarily in its cladding. The design strategies employed by OMA Asia reflect a "skin-based" methodology, which acknowledges the commercial realities of building in the real-estate-driven context of Hong Kong. Their cladding design for the AIA Tower assumes a "site" that is ten inches deep—the thickness of the building envelope.

AIA Tower is a straightforward rectangular extrusion with chamfered corners. It distinguishes itself through its cladding, which consists of alternating vertical bands of two different shades of blue glass. The mullion spacing and width of glass panels varies to create a random striped pattern during the day. An array of cold cathode lights integrated into the facade transforms the building at night, creating a spiraling neon spectacle.

In the words of architect Aaron Tan, "We took the most exciting and dynamic aesthetic element of Hong Kong—its neon urbanscape—as a graphic metaphor and wrapped our building in it."[1] The city of Hong Kong is abstracted and replicated in the skin of the building. By treating the city skyline as a "graphic landscape," OMA Asia sees high-rise design operating on the level of surface. And for the building itself, the incorporation of an urban phenomenon into its architectural expression suggests a compressed contextualism—belying a strategy of camouflage.

By internalizing the randomness found in the Hong Kong skyline, OMA Asia has created a microcosmic distillation, a strategy to both blend in and stand out. The AIA Tower holds a conceptual mirror up to the city, filters the image through its own architectural expression, and reproduces it in its own facades. The result is the skyscraper as multivalent urban figure, slipping effortlessly from foreground to background.

1 Aaron Tan, *Perspective*, Hong Kong, p. 20.

OMA Asia's AIA tower presents a new kind of camouflage contextualism. Its facades are made up of optical quotations from the city, abstracted and mapped onto the tower to allow it to blend into its context. The architects exploit the "thinness" of their design, limited to the building envelope, by celebrating the graphic potential of the facade. **OPPOSITE**: At night, a spiraling pattern of neon lights creates a controlled overlay of lighting patterns, and during the day, random bands of different blue glass break up the tower's bulk.

THE CENTRE
Dennis Lau & Ng Chun Man, Hong Kong, 1997

This building, sited in a dense neighborhood in Hong
Kong, is best known for its riotous, multicolored nighttime lighting display. Designed by local architects Dennis
Lau and Ng Chun Man, this 73-story, 997-foot (302
meter) pyramid-topped tower is modest by day and
spectacular by night.

The plan of the building consists of two rotated
squares, creating a multifaceted exterior expression
with eight corners. This simple design tactic doubles
the number of sought-after corner offices.

At the base, the building mass is lifted off the ground
to reveal its corner bracing members, expressing its
structure. A series of plazas and reflecting pools occupy
the ground floor of the complex. The openness of its
ground floor stands in sharp contrast to the densely built,
fine-grain texture of its urban context.

By day, the reflective-glass curtain wall is typical of
the mirrored urbanscape of Hong Kong. At night, the
facade is animated by thousands of cold cathode lights
that are integrated into the curtain wall, transforming
the building into a choreographed light show. The multicolored and pulsating tower becomes a pyrotechnic
architectural spectacle.

The perpetual spectacle of light and color epitomizes
Hong Kong's insatiable need for architectural novelty. Its
implications for the skyscraper as a form of mass media
suggest that the skyscraper has become a kind of holo-
graphic urban beacon.

The Centre's choreographed light show transforms the tower from a modest tower by day into a pulsating vertical spectacle by night.

Cheung Kong Centre's straightforward massing is offset by its intricate facade design. The facade consists of a dense weave of vertical and horizontal stainless-steel members, punctuated by a grid of light fixtures.

CHEUNG KONG CENTRE
Leo Daly with Cesar Pelli, Hong Kong, 1999

Built on the site of the former Hilton Hotel, the 951-foot (290 meter) Cheung Kong Centre occupies a site between the Bank of China and the Hongkong Shanghai Bank. The building's straightforward massing, a simple square-plan extrusion, belies the spectacle of the building's illuminated stainless-steel façade design.

The building is the headquarters for Cheung Kong Properties, one of Hong Kong's largest property developers. Determined to make a bold statement without sacrificing efficiency, Cheung Kong chairman Li Ka Shing gave the architects free reign on the design of the façades. The curtain wall design consists of reflective silver glass and a grid of stainless-steel tubular profiles. The daytime effect is a mirrored monolithic form beneath a glistening woven lattice.

At night, the tower is illuminated by thousands of fiber-optic points of light and by powerful spotlights evenly distributed over the facade. The spotlights illuminate the stainless-steel members and give the building a delicate metallic luminosity. The fiber-optic point lights can be programmed to generate animated effects like a giant, seventy-story pixilated LED screen. On special occasions such as Christmas and Chinese New Year, the tower transforms into a hallucinatory special-effects machine, producing giant animated graphics visible from miles away. Cheung Kong Centre epitomizes the idea that a skyscraper is a gigantic form of mass media. Legible at great distances, it broadcasts its indomitable presence.

Efficiently planned and spectacularly clad, Cheung Kong Centre epitomizes Hong Kong's obsession with the pragmatics of property development and the exuberance of image.

ecological

Ecological skyscrapers belong to an emerging area of design research in which the environmental impact of the building and issues of sustainability influence every scale and system of a tall building. Recent concerns with environmental issues have prompted skyscraper designs that employ a range of strategies to conserve energy, minimize buildings' impact on their surroundings, and ensure that the building materials used to construct them will be recyclable in the future. A few design firms are taking the lead in this area of design research, designing buildings in which the design's success or failure is determined by its relationship to the environment.

Malaysian architect Ken Yeang has written extensively about a bio-climactic approach to skyscraper design. Yeang's strategy is predicated on the idea that a building must be an integrated component of a local ecology.[1] Yeang's designs use both active and passive means to respond to a particular site with minimal detrimental impact on the context. Strategies include building configuration and orientation, the location of the service core, the design of the building envelope to incorporate sun shading, integrated plantings, and the use of natural ventilation.

fig 1 Garden within Norman Foster's Commerzbank.

New building technologies in facade design, mechanical systems, and new materials have impacted the design of ecological buildings. Architects have formed new collaborations with engineers to create integrated solutions. Helmut Jahn and Werner Sobek have coining the term "archineering" to describe their interdisciplinary collaboration that blurs the boundaries between architecture and engineering. Sobek, a Stuttgart-based engineer, and Jahn, a German-American architect, describe their practice as "innovative interdisciplinary exploration of the applied art of engineering" and "a total integration of architecture and engineering."[2] Collaborating with building energy specialists and framework planners, they have designed projects that utilize sophisticated engineering to allow buildings to be responsive to their climactic contexts. They imagine an architecture that takes constant readings of the local climactic conditions and adjusts itself accordingly, creating self-darkening facades, or facades that are capable of generating energy, or double-skinned facades that generate heat in the cavity with the aid of solar radiation. The incorporation of these technologies, they believe, will result in totally new solutions, and "an aesthetics that is itself dynamic and changeable."[3]

Environment refers to the interior environment as well as the exterior. Norman Foster has designed several buildings that employ double-skin curtain-wall systems and natural ventilation to provide ecologically sensitive office

177

environments. The designs create interior spaces that have qualities that make them comfortable, naturally lit, and ventilated, encouraging a sense of community. [fig 1]

As urban populations increase and cities continue to grow, careful urban planning must accompany economic planning. It is clear that high-density cities will continue to be part of any urban future, and that the skyscraper will continue to play a role in any city. Hong Kong's land scarcity and pragmatic high-density planning seems to be a case study for the high-density planning of future cities. Indeed, city planning in southern China follows a model developed in Hong Kong and exported to the north through investment and developments in the Pearl River Delta. These high-density new towns appear artificially dense in a region that does not share the land scarcity of Hong Kong. However, the Hong Kong model maintains that high-density levels in conjunction with infrastructure planning can create active urban centers, maintain property values, and allow for areas of undeveloped open space.

European architects seem to be leading the way in terms of sustainable design, partially because legislation in some European countries requires that building owners take on a more responsible attitude to energy consumption. Energy costs in Europe are higher than in the U.S., making the reduction of energy consumption a substantial reduction in the life cycle cost of a building, and making expensive first-cost systems viable investments. Within the projects in this volume, there are certainly different degrees of "ecological" buildings. A project like the Condé Nast Building in New York

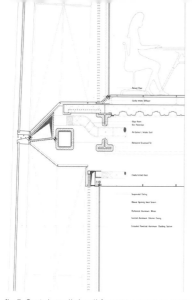

fig 3 Curtain wall detail from Norman Foster's Hearst Tower.

fig 4 Operable windows in a double-curtain wall are one strategy deployed in the SEG tower.

is a far cry from some European examples but remains significant as a benchmark in North American skyscraper design. Also, as each project is site- and climate-specific, it is interesting to note how strategies taken up by European architects are different from those engaged by architects working in the tropics.

It is clear that the future of architecture will involve the integration of environmental concerns with architectural design. Recent projects demonstrate design driven by environmental concepts alongside formal and social concerns. The range of styles that these buildings exhibit attest to the fact that environmental is not a style or formal category. Environmental design represents a consciousness towards issues, that when coupled with design strategies, produce structures that are dramatic as well as sustainable. The skyscraper as a discursive apparatus is a highly visible means to communicate an environmental consciousness.

1 Ken Yeang, *The Green Skyscraper, The Basis for Designing Sustainable Intensive Buildings*, Prestel, Munich, 1999.

2 Helmut Jahn, Werner Sobek, *Archi-neering*, Hatje Cantz Verlag, Leverkusen, 1999, pp. 12, 92.

3 Ibid., p. 94.

The sky gardens are distributed throughout the tower section.

COMMERZBANK HEADQUARTERS
Foster and Partners, Frankfurt, 1997

Norman Foster's Commerzbank Tower in Frankfurt is among the first of a new generation of ecological skyscrapers. The design strategy integrates the building into its ecological context with a minimal impact on the environment.

The triangular tower is designed so that offices at any level occupy only two sides of the floor plan. Four-story communal atrium gardens are located between the arms of the office spaces, creating a spiraling chain of interior gardens. The gardens become the visual and social focus for the office community clustered around the atrium. The atria bring daylight and fresh air into the central atrium, which acts as a natural convection chimney up the building for the inward-facing offices. The services and circulation cores are located in the corners with large *vierendeel* beams spanning between them, allowing the offices to be column-free.

Foster uses a botanical metaphor in describing the office spaces as "petals" and the central atrium as the "stem" unifying the form. Because the tower incorporates a fair amount of open space, the building mass is porous, creating the sense of openness and allowing for more natural air circulation and better daylight penetration. The curtain wall is designed with operable windows, allowing each individual to benefit from natural light and fresh air. This allows occupants to control their own environment for most of the year, and reduces energy consumption from redundant air conditioning.

While the tower has a distinctive presence on the Frankfurt skyline, it is also anchored into the more finely-scaled city fabric. It rises from the center of a historic city block alongside the original Commerzbank building. The design of the tower involved the restoration and careful rebuilding of some existing structures in order to integrate the tower into the city fabric. A public thoroughfare, housing restaurants and cafes, links the tower to the existing pedestrian networks.

The Commerzbank building contributed significantly to the awareness and growing demand for ecological high-rise buildings. In addition to reducing energy, the project also made advances in office-environment and workspace design.

The building design allows for lower energy consumption while providing comfortable working environments, as well as spaces that foster a sense of community.

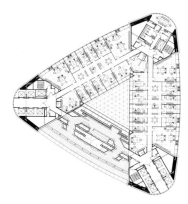

Offices occupy only two sides of the triangular floorplate, allowing the third side to open to multistory sky gardens. **RIGHT:** Commerzbank Headquarters sets a high standard for ecologically sensitive high-rise buildings while marking its presence on Frankfurt's skyline. **BELOW:** A sky garden.

MENARA UMNO
Hamzah & Yeang, Georgetown, 1998

The Menara UMNO building in Georgetown, Malaysia, designed by T. R. Hamzah & Yeang, embodies many of Dr. Ken Yeang's "green skyscraper" theories for the tropical high-rise building. The dynamically designed building is a built manifesto, a kind of polemical structure articulating the prescriptive strategies outlined by Yeang in his numerous publications.

The Menara UMNO building, completed in 1998, is a slender bar with a perimeter core on the south face. The shallow-office floorplates allow all areas to be within six meters of the facade, thus reducing the amount of artificial lighting required. The service-core volume takes the brunt of the southern solar gain, allowing the north-facing office areas to remain cooler. The lift lobbies, staircases, and restrooms employ natural light and ventilation. The office areas can be naturally ventilated, although the building is equipped with air conditioning. The facade design is "solar responsive," employing sun shades, blinds, and masks where they are required. The exposed frame of the tower and its disengaged massing allows for cross-ventilation and the introduction of some "vertical planting." The rooftop penthouse is shaded by an articulated canopy structure, providing additional solar protection.

The dynamic design of the building is not merely the outcome of an ecological strategy; it is highly expressive of its various building systems. Placement of the sun-screens on the facade is determined by solar orientation, but they also play an important aesthetic function. The mast and supergraphics are part of an architectural vocabulary that seeks to communicate the building's ecological functions.

Yeang's buildings are polemical artifacts. They are built manifestations of an emerging discourse on ecological buildings. As such, they communicate their functions through an expressive architectural language, which dramatizes the building's internal workings. Through its expressive design, the Menara UMNO building actively engages this debate on architecture and ecology.

Menara UMNO articulates ecological design principles through its expressive structure and building systems. **ABOVE:** A sail-like canopy structure shades the roof penthouse and encourages natural ventilation.

The mass of Menara UMNO is sculpted to encourage natural ventilation between the service core and the office volume.

CONDÉ NAST BUILDING
Fox & Fowle, New York, 1999

Built as part of the renaissance of Times Square, the Condé Nast building is also the first ecologically designed North American skyscraper. At the time of its construction, high-rise buildings rarely addressed environmental issues. Today, many of its innovations are considered standard for office buildings.

A monumental catalyst for the area, this is the first office building to be developed by the 42nd Street Development Corporation, a public/private consortium established to promote the redevelopment of Times Square. Located on the corner of 42nd Street and Broadway, the Condé Nast building straddles the glitzy Times Square entertainment area to the west and the corporate Midtown area to the east. Designed with two distinct faces, the west and north facades respond to Times Square with the glitter and technology of metal and glass, while the east and south facades respond to the corporate context with a historical stone facade, creating, according to the architect's description, a "marriage of pop culture and corporate dignity."

At street level, the tower's lobby, with its dramatically curved ceiling, connects 42nd and 43rd streets, drawing visitors through the building. Responding to the Times Square zoning ordinance, the building's base is covered with billboards and neon signage.

This building sets new standards in energy conser-vation, indoor environmental quality, recycling systems, and the use of sustainable materials. The large glazed-glass areas of curtain wall maximize daylight penetration. The curtain-wall glazing incorporates a low-E coating to filter out unwanted ultraviolet light while minimizing heat gain and loss. Photovoltaic panels are integrated in the spandrel areas on the upper floors of the east and south faces, generating a meager but symbolic amount of electricity by day.

Sophisticated mechanical systems ensure high indoor air quality by introducing filtered fresh air to the office environment. Tenant guidelines produced by the architects established environmental standards for lighting, power usage, furniture systems, carpet, fabrics, finishes, and maintenance materials to ensure indoor air quality, and also to serve as a comprehensive strategy to maintain environmental sustainability for the life of the building.

This pastiche of environmentalism, historicism, futurism, and commercialism creates a complex architectural organism. Indeed, the arguments for energy conservation seem out of place in a neighborhood like Times Square, which is predicated on a spectacular excess of energy-consuming visual pyrotechnics. A difficult first in the realm of ecological skyscraper design, it anticipates the next generation of ecologically sensitive North American skyscrapers.

The Condé Nast Building is the first North American skyscraper to employ environmentally sensitive design strategies, including power generation, recycled products, abundant natural light, and fresh air quality. The tower's facades contain integrated photovoltaic cells, producing largely symbolic amounts of solar power. **OPPOSITE:** Views from Times Square.

RWE HEADQUARTERS
Ingenhoven Overdiek und Partner, Essen, 1996

The glassy RWE Tower in the predominantly low-rise city of Essen, Germany, stands out due to its slender proportions and light materials, as well as its role as a pioneering work of sustainable design. Designed by the firm of Ingenhoven Overdiek und Partner, the tower utilizes sophisticated building systems, allowing it to consume less energy while still providing a comfortable, naturally lit and ventilated interior environment.

The cylindrical tower is sited in the middle of a landscaped park, surrounded by a lightweight pergola structure that defines the street edge. The tower itself consists of two volumes, the cylinder housing the office spaces and an adjacent elevator tower. The cylindrical plan allows all the offices to be located at the perimeter, guaranteeing access to natural light and air, while a service core and conference rooms occupy the center.

A "breathing double facade" system allows the occupants to benefit from natural light and air, without adding to the cooling and heating loads of the mechanical systems. The curtain wall is made up of a compartmentalized double layer of floor-to-ceiling glass. The outer layer is formed by a taut skin of low-iron glass (without the greenish tint) with an innovative horizontal mullion, which acts as an airflow valve and ventilates to the exterior. The compartments are accessible from the inside via sliding-glass doors, allowing occupants to control the amount of fresh air let in.

The building-management system monitors exterior climate data in relation to the interior temperature, and makes adjustments accordingly. Mechanized sun shades are integrated into the facade cavity and automatically raise or lower to control heat gain on the facade. Exterior sensors warn occupants to close their windows when it rains, or if it is particularly windy. Other systems allow for harvesting energy from roof-mounted photovoltaic panels.

Ingenhoven Overdiek und Partner describe their design criteria as "efficiency, ecological consciousness, economy of resource usage, and buildability." The RWE Headquarters is an example of an integrated-systems building that pioneered new technologies in facade design, energy efficiency, and sustainable materials. Its "smart-facade" system addresses the apparent conflict between thermal conservation and daylight illumination through the use of clear glass and integrated mechanical systems.

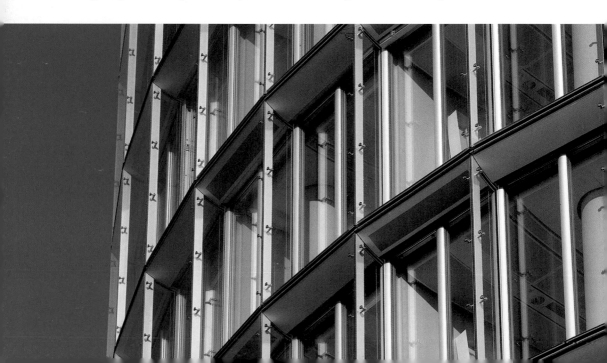

RWE Tower is a pioneering work of sustainable design, balancing energy consumption and interior occupant comfort with a striking form. **OPPOSITE:** The "intelligent glass facade" consists of double layers of clear glass, which allow natural light and air to enter, while providing a double thermal buffer.

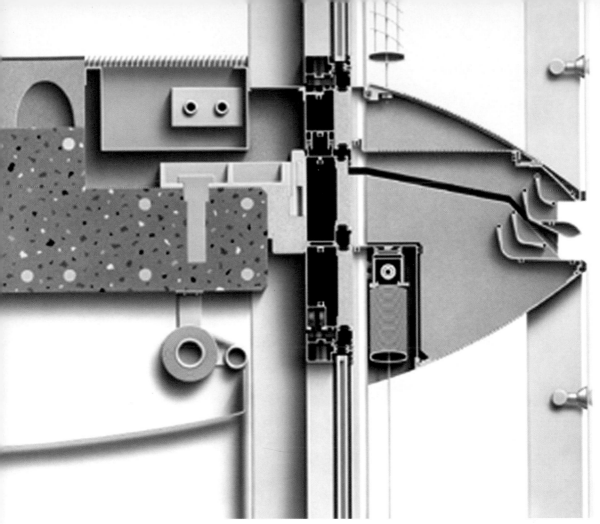

The "fish mouth" mullion which allows for a controlled flow of natural ventilation.

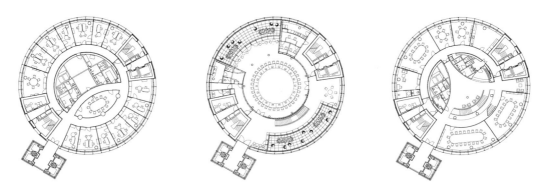

The tower's circular footprint and detached elevator core allows for a high percentage of perimeter offices.

Building section.

189

DEUTSCHE POST AG
Murphy/Jahn, Bonn, 2001

This sleek tower housing the new headquarters for the Deutsche Post is exemplary of a kind of sustainable design practice that achieves the goal of environmentally sensitive architecture without sacrificing aesthetics or occupant comfort. The tower rethinks the skyscraper as a building type by focusing on the integration of function, technology, and user comfort to create an architecture of "high technology and low energy."

The tower is made up of two curved semicircular masses connected by glass bridges. The connecting floors, at nine-story intervals, form atrium sky gardens, which are naturally ventilated and serve as interior communal spaces. A skylit annex houses additional public spaces at the base of the tower, and is clad in a "smart skin" of glass and integrated photovoltaic panels.

The facade design consists of a "twin-shell" glass curtain wall. The clear-glass outer shell allows for natural ventilation, and protects from rain, wind, and noise. The operable inner shell allows occupants to control the local interior climate. Floor-to-ceiling glazing optimizes daylight penetration and reduces energy consumption through the reduction of interior lighting, while integrated sun shades in the facade cavity control heat gain during periods of direct solar exposure. As the architects point out, the building's roof and facade are no longer surfaces with constant properties, but rather a highly specific system of interchangeable parts that allows the building to adapt to changes in temperature, humidity, light intensity, or acoustics. The architects describe the multi-cell roof as "the technical equivalent of the biological skin."

The building employs an integrated heating and cooling radiant-slab system, taking advantage of the thermal storage capacity of concrete. Additional heating and cooling systems assist with interior climate-control during summer and winter months.

Utilizing a computerized building-management system, the building monitors its climate and controls all of the components to optimize its "operational mode." The intelligent building creates its own equilibrium with the exterior environment through constant feedback. Careful monitoring reduces redundant lighting and conditioning, providing these only as required, and significantly reducing operating costs.

The collaboration between Jahn and Sobeek produces what they call "archi-neering," a seamless integration of architecture and engineering design. The design for the Deutsche Post building achieves new levels of design integration with technology, in order to create smarter and more responsible architecture. Jahn describes this environmental optimization by stating, "Nothing must be added, and nothing can be taken away."

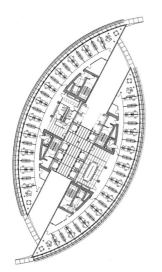 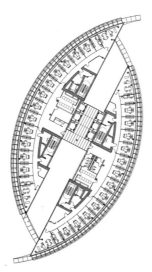 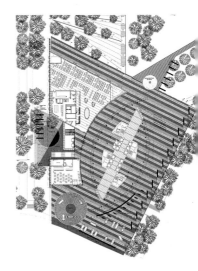

Semicircular office spaces flank a central atrium occupied by a naturally-ventilated interior atrium and the elevator core. **RIGHT:** Site plan.

Helmut Jahn's glassy Deutsche Post Tower marries architecture and engineering in what he calls "Archi-neering" a seamless integration of architecture and engineering design.

The glazed "loggias" behind the climate facade create communal spaces within the vertical section of the tower.

SEG APARTMENT TOWER
Coop Himmelb(l)au, Vienna, 1998

As with Coop Himmelb(l)au's other work, the design of the SEG Tower is inspired by the dynamic nature of the cloud. Constantly shifting and ephemeral, the cloud serves as an appropriate model for this dramatically sculpted ecological tower. The angular geometry of the tower's sloped south facade expresses the architects' interest in dynamic flexible forms, but also acts as the "climate facade."

The building consists of two buildings stacked on top of each other, one commercial and one residential. Common spaces occupy the "sky lobby" zone in between, which houses a playground, a "teleworking café," and a sun deck. The residential tower contains stacked units that cluster around interior atrium spaces. Clusters of units form a sense of community around a series of glazed loggias. The introduction of semi-public areas throughout the tower reinforces the idea of the skyscraper as a vertical community.

The sloped-glass "climate facade," which screens a series of multistory semi-public loggias, forms a thermal buffer to the outside. The operable windows in the climate facade allow residents the ability to con-trol their environment and regulate their connection to the outside. The tower also employs a "passive energy concept" to store thermal energy produced during daylight hours in a thermal reservoir located in the interior of the building. In the winter, spring, and autumn, this thermal energy is recirculated to reduce the amount of total energy consumption.

The dramatically sculpted SEG Tower is an example of the convergence of bold design and sensitive ecological considerations, creating an architecture in which it is comfortable to live and work, while simultaneously limiting the building's impact on the environment. Ecological design involves high capital investment in the architecture, which pays off over the life of the building through reduced operating costs. Unlike a speculative office building, where return on investment drives most decisions, residential buildings like the SEG Tower are designed to target a market of homebuyers whose interests are compatible with sustainable sensibilities. The environmentally conscious design generates its own value, as society reevaluates the importance of sustainability.

The dramatic sloped facade screens of SEG Tower are internal semi-public spaces in this ecologically sensitive design for a residential tower.

193

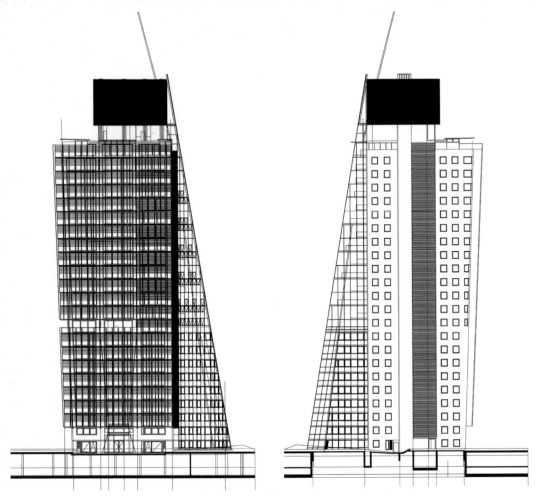

The building sections illustrate the stepped profile of "semi-public" spaces behind the sloped facade.
BELOW: Illustration of an operable window in the double-skin glass wall.

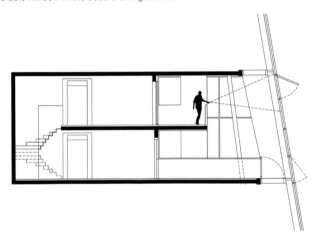

The "climate facade" is also the building's primary public face.

195

GSW ADMINISTRATION BUILDING
Sauerbruch Hutton Architekten, Berlin, 1999

The new headquarters for GSW is a colorful addition to a part of Berlin that straddles the former division between East and West. The project is an assemblage of five distinct elements, employing a strategy of collage to incorporate an existing office building. This strategy seems particularly suited for a part of the city that bears the traces of a complex and violent history.

The project is made up of the original building, a concave slab, a low podium bar, and an elliptical figure perched on the bar. The original building, dating from 1961, is integrated into the composition, becoming one of the elements in the new complex. The concave slab is the most striking part of the composition. Its west facade is covered in colorful orange, pink, and red sunscreens. The lower bar is clad in charcoal-gray tiles and the oval structure is clad in brightly colored metal panels. The lower structures define the perimeter of the site and maintain the low scale of the existing urban fabric. The new slab sails above the perimeter bars and addresses the larger urban scale.

The project is designed with a "low-energy concept," which allows the building to employ natural ventilation instead of artificial air conditioning. The narrow footprint of the concave bar allows optimized daylight use, and encourages natural cross-ventilation. The facade systems on the west and east faces are designed to be operable and solar-responsive, to encourage natural ventilation through a double facade on the west and operable louvers on the east. Fresh air enters each floor on the east facade via operable ventilation louvers. On the west facade, the colorful sunscreen panels in the cavity block out direct sunlight, and louvers at the bottom draw fresh air in from below. The warm air is vented at the top and is kept circulating due to natural convection. A surfboard-shaped "wind roof" crowns the slab. Its aerodynamic form protects the cavity from rain, and also encourages the natural stack effect in the west facade.

The colorful sunscreens on the west facade create a lively mosaic that animates the facade and registers the movements of its elements by the occupants. Visible from great distances, the GSW Building displays the interactivity of the structure and its systems, performing a critical function for ecological design—communicating its environmental strategies on its facades.

An operable mosaic, the west facade is made up of a double-glass convection facade with colorful sun shading panels. **RIGHT:** The view from the east with the existing tower in the foreground.

ADIA HEADQUARTERS
Kohn Pedersen Fox International, Abu Dhabi, 2004

The curvilinear headquarters building for the Abu-Dhabi Investment Authority (ADIA) combines a sensuous formal vocabulary with a low-energy design strategy appropriate to the Middle Eastern climate. The building mass is draped in a glass curtain wall that folds in and out of the tower, transforming from the taut skin of the exterior envelope to the inner liner of the internal atrium.

The building is sited in a green fringe of the city, close to the sea. Its curved form gestures to the waterfront on the west, with elevators and other services concentrated on the east. The tower consists of two wings connected by an elevator core and a setback atrium. The building mass is camouflaged by the undulating ribbonlike surface that projects above the tower, culminating in a sail-like projection on the north facade.

The curtain wall consists of a double facade of clear glass that admits natural light and air while cutting down on the amount of solar heat gain. The taut glass skin transforms on the west facade with the introduction of horizontal sun-shading devices. The interior atrium is conceived as a series of stacked sky-gardens that act as passive means to regulate humidity and temperature, as well as contributing to a sense of community.

The architects describe the form of the tower as a "rethinking of the tall office building in a changing cultural, social, and environmental context." The organic form of the tower seems to be derived from a concern with the fluid forces in the context, rather than a rigorous internal logic. Indeed the curvilinear geometry of the floor departs from conventional space-planning modularity. The combination of bold sculptural form and sensitive environmental systems makes the tower a benchmark in the ecological design of the skyscraper.

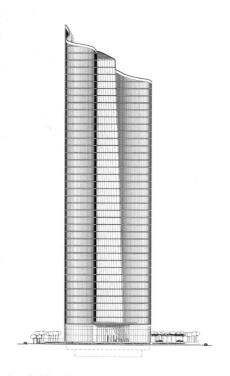

Building elevation.

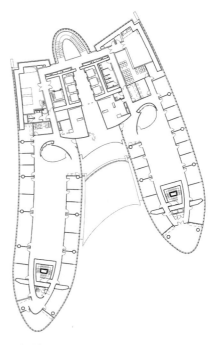

The typical floorplan illustrates the tower's curvilinear geometry.
OPPOSITE: The ADIA Headquarters combines a sensual formal vocabulary of folding surfaces with a low-energy design strategy suited to the local climate.

110 BISHOPSGATE
Kohn Pedersen Fox International,
London, 2005

The building section illustrates the composition of the tower as a series of stacked atria flanked by office spaces.

110 Bishopsgate is part of a new generation of high-rise buildings approved for construction in the City of London. The environmentally sensitive and structurally articulated tower is expressive of the technologies that enable it.

The project is located on the eastern edge of the old city, on a prominent site at the junction of Bishopsgate & Camomile Street, and across the street from the Georgian church of St. Botolph. It forms part of a cluster of office buildings that includes the NatWest Tower and the 30 St. Mary Axe. The recent crop of office buildings in London corresponds to a demand for large floorplates to provide flexible office space in the center city. It also responds to the evolution in expectations of what a contemporary office building should be with regard to the working environment that it creates and the approach to energy consumption and sustainability.

A perimeter service core on the south organizes the building, allowing open plan offices to benefit from exposure to the west, north, and east. The service core acts as a buffer against solar exposure to the south, while allowing for continuous and unobstructed working spaces on the north side. Responding to the technical and social demands of the modern workplace, the building is organized as a vertical armature of flexible spaces. Office spaces are clustered around multistory atria that the architects call "villages," allowing tenants flexibility in renting either a single floor or multiple floors connected by internal stairs. Other amenities include retail and restaurant spaces at grade and a public restaurant at roof level.

The east and west facades, clad in clear glass, allow occupants to control the amount of fresh air ventilation, while reducing the amount of solar heat gain in through the glass. The building's structural skeleton is expressed on its north facade, framing the atria.

Designed by Kohn Pedersen Fox International, the firm's London office, 110 Bishopsgate represents the translation and adaptability of the high-rise office building type to central London and the implementation of demands for flexible space as well as environmental sensitivity.

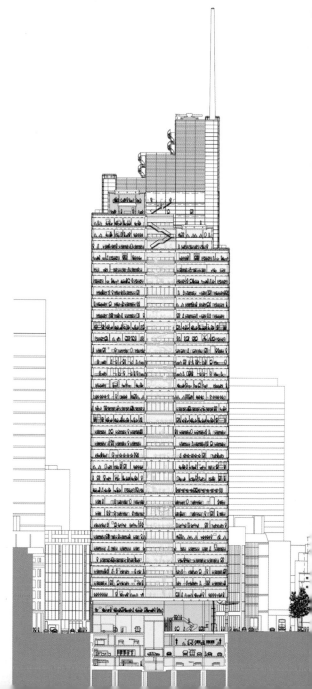

The environmentally sensitive 110 Bishopsgate is part of a new generation of office buildings planned for the City of London.

ELEPHANT & CASTLE ECO-TOWER
T.R. Hamzah & Yeang, London, 2010

The Eco-Tower forms the centerpiece of the Elephant & Castle redevelopment in London, set for completion in the year 2010. The thirty-five-story residential tower, designed by Malaysian architect Kenneth Yeang, introduces environmental concepts for high-rise buildings developed in Asia to a European context.

The slender tower is split in two volumes that embrace a central naturally ventilated sky court between them. Communal facilities and sky gardens are distributed throughout the tower, transforming it into a small "vertical city." Shops, restaurants, bars, sports facilities, and playgrounds supplement the mix of apartment uses to create a diversely programmed mixed-use skyscraper.

The tower employs a number of low-energy concepts. The porosity of the tower encourages natural ventilation to cool apartment units. Operable windows in the double-glazed facade allow occupants to regulate the amount of fresh air according to the building's mechanical mode, which ranges from passive to mixed, to full and productive. Mechanical systems can be calibrated to provide the appropriate balance of services depending on the season.

Eco-Tower demonstrates that environmental design involves a conscious effort on the part of architects to work at the scale of the master plan and the scale of the detail. Eco-Tower's integrated design approach combines infrastructure planning, building programming, landscaping, and facade detailing. Yeang's inventive design approach creates new "land uses," as a kind of vertical master plan. His efforts to rethink and diversify the building type produce new models for the design of the ecological skyscraper.

Elephant & Castle Eco-Tower demonstrates an environmental design strategy applied at a range of scales, from master plan to facade detail. **OPPOSITE:** The open lattice structure of the Eco-Tower provides a porous armature into which residential units have been inserted.

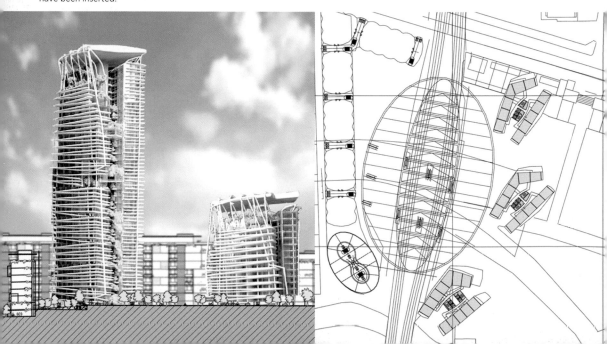

In the aftermath of the terrorist attacks of September 11, 2001, debates centered on how to rebuild New York and on the role architecture would play in the process of reconstruction and memorialization. Some groups have called for the site to remain empty as a memorial park; others have argued for a vigorous rebuilding effort, bigger and taller than before. All groups agree that a unique memorial is necessary on the site, now considered hallowed ground.

The tragic events precipitated a collective questioning of the symbolic importance of the structures that we erect: their mythological stature, their emotional impact, their power, and their vulnerability. The design proposals for the site reflect varied responses to the tragedy; however, all share a belief that architecture can embody collective aspirations and can respond appropriately to extreme events.

The debate has also raised questions about the symbolic function that architecture plays in representing a corporation, a city, or a nation. Some critics have argued that the age of the skyscraper is over, that building towers as monuments to greed and ego is inappropriate. Others argue that skyscrapers are not safe in extreme events, and that changes are required in building codes to ensure occupant safety. Others have attempted to reimagine the building type, producing unique designs as a response to an unprecedented event.

A group of artists and designers, including architects John Bennett and Gustavo Bonevardi of PROUN Space Studio, artists Julian LaVerdiere and Paul Myoda, architect Richard Nash Gould, and lighting designer Paul Marantz, created the "Tribute in Light," a pair of light projections that formed the spectral profiles of endless towers. Visible from miles around, the light towers created

Eric Owen Moss proposed memorial park marks the absence of
the World Trade Center towers by tracing their shadows at the
moment of impact and the moment of collapse. **PREVIOUS
PAGE:** The Tribute in Light towers recreated the towers as
beams of light rising from Lower Manhattan. Seen from various
locations around New York, the Tribute in Light towers transformed depending on perspective and atmospheric conditions.

an ephemeral presence in the void left by the World Trade Center. In the words of a member of the design team, "Light takes solid form."

Invited by galleries, magazines, and institutions, various artists and architects have created proposals for the World Trade Center site. These designs range from green parks, deep voids, and reflecting pools, to rebuilding the towers in voluptuous new forms. Some proposals rejected the idea of building anything on the site at all. Several proposals yielded thoughtful reinterpretations of the skyscraper and its relationship to the city, as well as its function as a dynamic symbol of reconstruction and recovery.

Eric Owen Moss's proposal for a monument creates a park that occupies the footprints of the towers' shadows at the moment of impact, and then again at the moment of collapse. The shadows of the absent towers mark their presence spatially, as well as temporally. Moss's poetic response to the events refuses to create form, but rather marks an absence. The Max Protetch Gallery exhibited Moss's design for the memorial park in late 2001, as part of a larger exhibit.

A proposal by Boston-based Office d'A proposes an organic skyscraper that transforms from base to top. The design, also exhibited by the Max Protetch Gallery, is a commentary on the building type as well as the particular site. The Office d'A proposal creates a new form for the skyscraper. The proposal blurs the distinction between base, middle, and top; it also discards the conventional notions of repetition and modularity that are the formal genesis of the skyscraper and the original World Trade Center in favor of an irregular complexity in building modules made possible through new computer-aided manufacturing techniques. Office d'A's proposal advocates a vigorous rebuilding and a critical reassessment of the skyscraper as a building form.

Zaha Hadid's scheme, commissioned by *New York* magazine architectural critic Joseph Giovannini, envisions two new twin towers to be built on the site, while preserving the footprints of the originals. The sinuous forms of the towers would house residential and office functions. Hadid explains the transformation of the towers: "The floorplates swell and recede along the vertical axis, expressing the principle of variation rather than repetition." The proposal is a strong affirmation of the need to rebuild and to do so in a spectacular way, with skyscraper designs that defy building types and precedents. The proposals offer a glimpse at the recently unimagined future of the skyscraper.

After months of controversy, exhibited plans, public hearings, and journalistic outcry, the Lower Manhattan Development Corporation solicited designs from several architectural teams to produce designs that would result in a plan for the World Trade Center site. The designs were presented in a public forum, broadcast live on television and radio. The general public participated in the process and followed the presentations in an unprecedented way.

A design presented by Norman Foster proposes two polyhedral towers that spring from distinct bases and transform as they rise to "kiss" at the top. The design replaces the original towers with a new pair of twins, creating another set of iconographic towers on the same site. The new towers are derived from a logic of triangulated structures that are inherently stable and derived from forms found in nature. The scheme also introduced concepts of ecological design in their proposal, making the case for intelligent building systems and renewable energy sources.

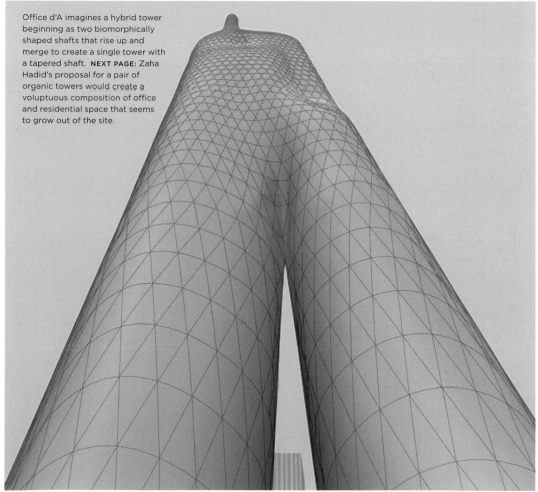

Office d'A imagines a hybrid tower beginning as two biomorphically shaped shafts that rise up and merge to create a single tower with a tapered shaft. **NEXT PAGE:** Zaha Hadid's proposal for a pair of organic towers would create a voluptuous composition of office and residential space that seems to grow out of the site.

Several designs were submitted by teams of architects, some in collaboration with artists and landscape architects. A team led by Skidmore, Owings & Merrill consisted of Field Operations, Michael Maltzan, SANAA, Iñigo Manglano-Ovalle, Rita McBride, Tom Leader, Jessica Stockholder, and Elyn Zimmerman. Their scheme consists of a dense grid of nine slender towers evenly distributed across the site and all rising to the same height. The towers lean and bend as they rise, giving the impression of organic growth rather than commercial office space. A series of ramps and bridges connects the shafts incorporating parks and public spaces to replace the open space that previously existed on the site.

A proposal by Richard Meier, Peter Eisenman, Charles Gwathmey, and Steven Holl creates a pair of latticelike towers that screen the site from the north and east and gesture to the footprints of the former World Trade Center. The lattice, made up of vertical shafts and horizontal bridges, envisions a hybrid building type composed of office, hotel, residential, and recreational uses. Their proposal also envisions a memorial square as a pedestrian zone extending from the site of the original towers and spreading out into Lower Manhattan. The monolithic structures are both brutally simple and strangely poetic; their cantilevered horizontal bars gesture towards each other "like the fingers of a pair of hands."

United Architects, a collaboration of a younger generation of architects from around the globe includes Greg Lynn, Kevin Kennon, Reiser + Umemoto, Foreign Office Architects, Imaginary Forces, and UN Studio. Intent on rethinking the possibilities of architecture on the site, United Architects proposed a single building morphed out of a cluster of buildings to create a concave grouping of stalk-like shafts. The faceted structure gestures to a memorial on the footprints of the original towers, "like the vaulting of a cathedral." A proposed "skyway" at the top of some of the lower portions would link the structure together and create a new kind of elevated public space.

THINK, a group of architects including Rafael Viñoly, Frederic Schwartz, Shigeru Ban, and landscape architect Ken Smith, initially submitted three proposals, one of which, their World Cultural Center, was selected as a possible direction. Inspired by the Eiffel Tower, the third THINK proposal consists of a pair of hollow towers—open, cylindrical structures that house a series of cultural facilities suspended within the structural web. The footprints of the original World Trade Center are recreated as parks, suspended at a height equivalent to their original height. A museum, education and conference center, and performing-arts centers would also be housed in the lattice structure.

Studio Daniel Libeskind's scheme was selected in February 2003 to serve as the basis for the rebuilding efforts. Daniel Libeskind, best known for his signature fragmentary formal language and pondering of theoretical framing, proposed a scheme that was generated by the need to create a memorial to the event. Libeskind's Jewish Museum in Berlin interprets the tragedy of the Holocaust in the jagged forms of the building and its enigmatic voids. For the World Trade Center site, Libeskind's plan consists of an ensemble of angular towers and shards arrayed around the footprints of the World Trade Center towers. A zone, designated as the "wedge of light," is located so that on the anniversary of the attacks, the space is bathed in shadow-free sunlight. Libeskind's gesture towards the memorial is to preserve the foundation walls of the tower, almost as open wounds. The final outcome for the site remains to be seen.

WORLD TRADE CENTER PROPOSALS, LMDC COMPETITION 2003

RICHARD MEIER, PETER EISENMAN, CHARLES GWATHMEY, STEVEN HOLL

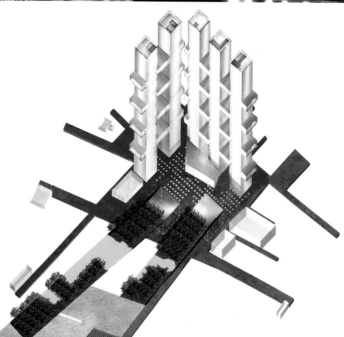

RICHARD MEIER, PETER EISENMAN, CHARLES GWATHMEY, STEVEN HOLL 225

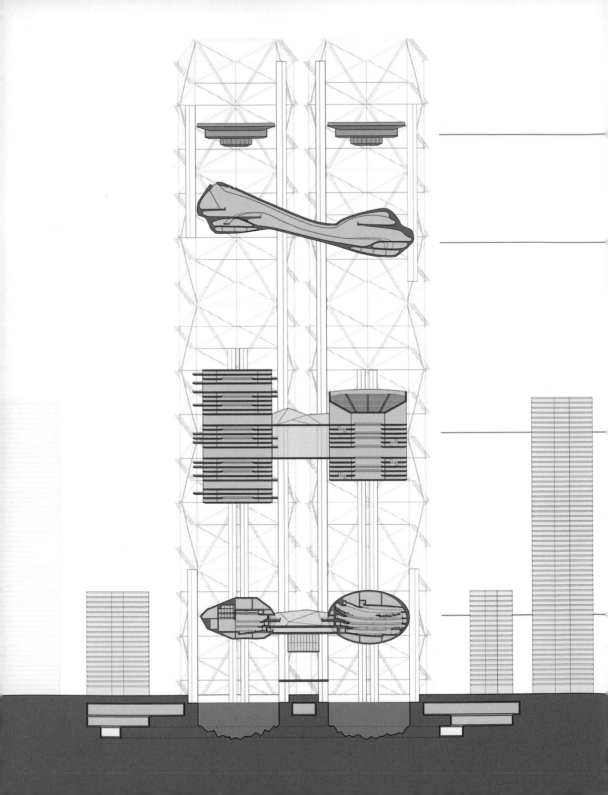

MEMORIAL
PROMENADE

WEST STREET

MEMORIAL
PROMENADE

SLURRY WALL

GREENWICH
STREET

VIEW TO
GROUND ZERO

SEPTEMBER 11
PLACE

LINE OF HOPE

TOWER 1

LINE OF HOPE

ENGINE COMPANY 10 LADDER 9

GROUND ZERO
MEMORIAL SITE

TOWER 2 FOOTPRINT

RO MEMORIAL SITE

I am indebted to a large number of people who have encouraged, inspired, provoked, and engaged.

Working with Stephen Case and Juliette Cezzar on the book was both enjoyable and illuminating. Thanks for their patience and insight.

I owe a special thanks to the architects and photographers, whose work is presented here.

I'd like to thank William Pedersen for his generous introduction, and for an extended conversation about the design of high-rise buildings. I am greatly indebted to everyone at Kohn Pedersen Fox for providing a context where design and large-scale architecture are rigorously engaged. I am especially grateful to Paul Katz for having confidence in me and for sharing his experience and insights. Others at KPF who shared a great deal of wisdom and experience include, Andreas Hausler, Glen Dacosta, John Lucas, Tom Holzmann, Paul Pichardo, Russell Paterson, Jerri Smith, Roger Robison, Gene Kohn, Jamie von Klemperer, William Louie, Michael Greene, Bob Cioppa, Rob Whitlock, Ming Leung, Tomas Alvarez, Duncan Reid, and Craig Nealy. I also owe a special thanks to Ian Luna.

For an excellent education in high rise design, I am grateful to Jim Robinson, Mike Arnold, Victor Meakins, of Hongkong Land, Mr. N. H. Sitt and Ringo Chu of Sun Hung Kai Properties, Adrian Hardwick Jones of Aedas LPT, Mr. W. H. Lam, Thomas Tsang, of Wong & Ouyang, Joe Khoury of ALT, Leslie Robertson of LERA, and David Scott and Ricardo Pittela of Arup.

Other friends that have sustained an ongoing conversation and debate include, Ashley Schafer, John Shnier, Amanda Reeser, Mark Pasnik, An Te Lu, Lihi Gerstner, Charles Renfro, Donald Shillingburg, Flavio Stigliano, Dean Simpson, Michael Arad, Bruno Caballé, Gene Miao, Liz Austin, Chris Deckwitz, Marisa Yiu, Christian Lemon, Karel Klein, Paul Baird, Andrew Kawahara, Rena Gyftopolous, Fanny Lee, Chris Palumbo, Julia Lau, Bernard Chang, Tony Song, Laurent Gutierrez and Valerie Portefaix. Special thanks to John Butlin who took many of the striking photographs of Hong Kong.

Thanks also to the individuals who facilitated the process: Richard Dubrow, Jon Kletzien (Advanced Media Design), Alan MacDonald, Fraser MacDonald (Architech Animation); Winka Dubbeldam, Michael Hundsnurscher (Archi-Tectonics); Anthony Rimore, Dennis Wilhelm (Arquitectonica); Caroline Nutley (The Art Institute of Chicago); Elizabeth Safford (Art Resource); Tom Wright (Aktins); Rosario Beck (Santiago Calatrava); Gabriella Wilson Sadler (Atelier Christian de Portzamparc); Charlotte Kruk (Ateliers Jean Nouvel); Philip Brown; Mig Halpine, Lesley Holford (Cesar Pelli); Ursula Haberle (Coop Himmelb(l)au); Karina Kabigting (Corbis); Andrea Wohl (Costas Kondylis); May Chen (C. Y. Lee); Matthew Banister (dbox); Dennis Lau, Ng Chun Man; Stephanie Grandjacques, Nora Vorderwinkler (Dominique Perrault); Cynthia Davidson, Larissa Babij (Eisenman Architects); Hannah Slama (Eric Owen Moss); Erica Stoller (Esto); Sarah Crouch, Stuart Smith, Barbra Albers (Ellerbe Becket); Elizabeth Walker (Foster and Partners); Kirsten Sibilia, Bill Chalkley (Fox & Fowle); Dr. Ken Yeang, Andy Chong (Hamzah & Yeang); Robert Shimmer (Hedrich Blessing); Ute Einhoff (Ingenhoven Overdiek); Ellis Katz, Matther Skarr (John Portman & Associates); Catherine Chase (Kevin Roche John Dinkeloo); Elizabeth Austin, Gail Cheney (Kohn Pedersen Fox); K. Y. Cheung, John Lee, Steve Gertner (Lee Timchula); Sandy Zanella, Michelle Hansen, Michelle Bryant, Lisa Splichal (MGM Mirage); Keith Palmer, Lori Hladek (Murphy/Jahn); Eileen Morales, Marguerite Lavin, (Museum of The City of New York); Bonnie Duncan, Rick Buckley (NBBJ); Gayle Webber (Norr Group); Nader Terani, Tali, (Office d'A); Nico Glade, Jan Knikker, (OMA); Carlos Ott; Janet Adams, Dwidson Meyer, (Pei Cobb Freed and Partners); Pietro Filardo (Philip Johnson); Aaron Tan, Charles Cheng (RAD, OMA Asia); Stefania Canta, Chiara Casazza (Renzo Piano Building Workshop); Alfonso D'onofrio, Lisetta Koe (Richard Meier and Partners); Ambrose Tang (Rocco Design Limited); Heide Hendricks (Ruder Finn); Karine Stigt (Sauerbruch Hutton); Pam Kane, Elizabeth Geiger (Skidmore Owings & Merrill); Joan Nelson (The Stubbins Associates); Rob Claiborne (Studio Daniel Libeskind); Steven Weinberg (Transamerica Corporation); Machteld Kors (United Architects); Alda Ly (Rafael Viğnoly); Andy Whiting; Montserrat Mari Gili (Zaha Hadid).

I thank my parents for all their love and enthusiasm over the years.

Thanks to J. Meejin Yoon.

Illustration Credits

World Trade CTR